"Vidal's best book!"

—Associated Press

_____

In **TWO SISTERS** you will find a novel, a movie and, above all, brilliant, incisive comments on everything and everyone (from Jackie to Jack Kerouac) under the sun.

_____

"Worthy of America's finest essayist."

—New Statesman

Two Sisters

A Memoir in the Form of a Novel

by Gore Vidal

BANTAM BOOKS · LONDON · NEW YORK · TORONTO

A NATIONAL GENERAL COMPANY

TWO SISTERS
*A Bantam Book/published by arrangement with
Little, Brown and Company*

PRINTING HISTORY
*Little, Brown edition published July 1970
Bantam edition published September 1971*

*Sections of this book first appeared in the May 1970
issue of* ESQUIRE
*Sections of the book appeared in the Winter 1970
issue of* PARTISAN REVIEW

*Bantam Books are published by Bantam Books, Inc., a National
General company. Its trade-mark, consisting of the words "Bantam
Books" and the portrayal of a bantam, is registered in the United
States Patent Office and in other countries. Marca Registrada.
Bantam Books, Inc., 666 Fifth Avenue, New York, N.Y. 10019.*

PRINTED IN THE UNITED STATES OF AMERICA

For N. A. Steers

*Si le monde se plaint de quoy je parle trop de moy,
je me plains de quoy il ne pense seulement pas à soy.*

—Montaigne, *Du Repentir*

TWO SISTERS

NOW

Despite my protests, Marietta revealed her breasts.

"You would never know—well, *you* would, but no one else—that I shall be fifty-two years old this November. Sagittarius, what else? That's why we get on so well. Cancer always does with Sagittarius."

"Libra." As I gazed without lust at those familiar not altogether fallen breasts, they suddenly resembled scales, my birth sign made absurdly flesh.

"They still look awfully nice. But I think you'd better cover up." I indicated the building opposite. The sight of her had frozen two plasterers at their work: the scales had become the minatory eyes of Medusa.

"You were always such a prude." With a brisk shake, reminiscent of her old friend Isadora Duncan, she returned the relics of our past association to her blouse. Released from Marietta's spell, one workman dropped a bucket and looked to heaven for a sign while the other, eyes shut, gripped his genitals—in Italy a common gesture and not, as foreigners think, a sign of lewdness or lice but a way of touching base in order to ward off the evil eye.

Marietta often has that effect on men. It is no accident that her favorite adjective is *ensorcelled*. She cannot write a book without it. Unfortunately I cannot read a book that contains it (excepting always the handsome prose of Anaïs Nin). This has made for a degree of coolness between us since Marietta wants to be not only a love goddess (a legend in her own time, as the reviewers say—as, in fact, she herself has so often noted in the five volumes of memoirs she has to date given us)

1

but an artist of the first rank, heiress to Sappho, George Sand, Virginia Woolf, a colossa of literature whose shadow falling across the waste land of twentieth century art makes sickly pale those contemporaries who must dwell forever in her shade, particularly Mary McCarthy, Carson McCullers and Marietta's near-contemporary Katherine Anne Porter.

Marietta Donegal is sixty-eight not fifty-two; yet in her way she is still beautiful, preserved by an insatiable appetite for glory and sex. Alone among the women of our time, Marietta has managed to domesticate Sophocles' cruel and insane master. At eighty she will be making love and writing about it in that long autobiography which begins with our century and will, I am certain, last well into the next for like it or not, we live in *her* age—was she not the mistress of D. H. Lawrence (two volumes hardly described the three—or was it four?—times she bedded that ensorcelled genius) as well as the beloved inspiration—and brutal seducer—of so many other writers, painters, sculptors and even one President, though whether it was sunrise or sunset at Campobello has never been entirely clear (out of admiration for Eleanor Roosevelt she has yet to give us the entire story). She is unique in all but talent.

"I could hardly believe it when I heard you'd written *Myra Breckinridge*. It was so out of character."

After a quarter century of publication, I have learned never to discuss my work with other writers. It excites them too much. I shifted Marietta's attention to Nabokov's *Ada* which had just been published. I half expected her to tell me that she had been his muse, too, but apparently they had not met. I was not surprised to learn that his current vogue distressed her, as it does us all (writers are by nature envious, and easily undone: is there *no* justice?), even though the success of men writers usually does not upset her quite as much as that of women. Shortly after an entire issue of *Horizon* had been devoted to Mary McCarthy's "The Oasis," the two girls met by accident at Martha's Vineyard. With a terrible cry, Marietta fainted from rage.

"I was so upset by what Nabokov said about you in *Time*."

"I'm afraid I don't read *Time*."

This is not true. I am addicted to *Time*'s political "reporting" in which one can follow from week to week the fictional adventures of actual people. Instead of decently ending, the novel seems to have got a new lease upon our attention in the form of the weekly "news" magazine.

"Nabokov attacked everyone. Tolstoi. You. Mailer."

"Ah, that old world charm . . ."

"Charm! I find it disgusting."

"But normal. Writers like to attack their betters."

This was a mistake. Inadvertently, I had left an opening which she was capable of filling; happily, Czarist Russia's gift to our poor letters continued to distract her. "He attacked *Portnoy's Complaint* . . ."

"That was unkind. I should have thought the man who celebrated pedophilia would regard masturbation with a tolerant eye."

". . . and said that even *you* were more interesting than Philip Roth."

"That was perceptive."

"But you know what he *meant*."

"I still enjoy his books. Oh, perhaps not as much as he does. That would be impossible but . . ."

"How easily taken in Americans are! They are mad for foreigners who make fun of them."

"Don't worry. No one will ever read *Ada*."

"It is already a best seller."

"And has taken its historic place beside *By Love Possessed*, *Ship of Fools*, and *The Confessions of Nat Turner*. Books that defy one to read them, in just the way the Sunday *New York Times* does. They are ceremonial artifacts to be displayed but not used." I was launched upon a favorite theme. Also, in the back of my mind, the perfect analogy to Nabokov had suddenly surfaced. James Branch Cabell. I began to compose a blurb. "Not since Cabell's *Jurgen* has there been a novel so certain to delight the truly refined reader as Nabokov's *Ada*."

But Marietta was on her own tack. "*The Heart's Archery* hasn't sold twenty thousand copies since March."

"The what?"

Marietta's eyes became hard malachite. The voice dropped an octave. "My last book of memoirs. I sent it to you. You never answered."

"I never got it." This was true. "There is no such thing as a mail service in Rome. Do you know how many sacks of mail there are at San Silvestro?"

The subject did not intrigue her. "You're in the book, you know." She sounded threatening. "That party in Los Angeles. Isherwood's in it, too."

Marietta was one of the first to realize that in an age of total publicity personality is all that matters. And if one has "mattered" in the world, by middle age one is sure to have figured in a dozen novels, a hundred memoirs, a thousand newspaper stories. I have already made a number of appearances under my own name in Marietta's memoirs where, inevitably, I say something disagreeable which she gets slightly wrong. Yet, sexually, she is surprisingly coy. Her lovers—if alive—are only embedded, as it were, in her fiction. The three months we lived together in 1947 (I twenty-two, she forty-seven) formed the central motif to one of her most Lorenzian novels in which I appear as a faun-faced poet, so overwhelmed by her autumnal beauty and ripe wisdom as to contract an acute case of priapism. At least that is Marietta's version. My recollection is that I was tired a good deal of the time (I was coming down with hepatitis) but enjoyed being with her at the Hôtel de l'Université in Paris for a summer (in 1947 it was always summer) because she had a gift for intimacy. She was—is?—one of those rare women with whom one likes to talk after the act. *Post coitum Marietta* I once called her. I don't think she was pleased.

As we sat on my terrace overlooking all of Rome to the west of the Largo Argentina, a fine if jumbled view of golden buildings, one twisted tower (Borromini's St. Ivo), the green Gianicolo and a dozen domes, the nearest Sant' Andrea della Valle (*Tosca* Act One), the farthest St. Peter's like a gray-ridged skull, Marietta discussed the latest details of her literary career. I shall not record what she said since she is bound to confide it to us in Volume Six of her memoirs.

At first I could not figure out what she wanted. True, she still expects me to compose a full-scale critique of her work in which, once and for all, her quality is established. For twenty years we have played this game, she cajoling, threatening, weeping. I backing and filling, evading the dread commitment. I had assumed when she rang me this morning to say she was in Rome and needed my advice that, once again, I would be asked, first, to write about her at length or, failing that, to praise in a line or two the . . . what was the title? *The Heart's Archery*. But the expected request was not made. She had something else on her mind.

"Eric Van Damm. You remember him, don't you? From Paris."

A long shut door swings open to reveal high summer —yes, it was always summer twenty years ago. I am standing in a room at the Hôtel de l'Université as Eric, tall, slender, blond, quite naked, takes apart for the hundredth time his German movie camera. That moment has remained as vivid to me as Henry James's recollection after a half century of a boy cousin being sketched in the nude at Newport before his life was "cut short, in a cavalry clash, by one of the Confederate bullets of 1863."

Death, summer, youth—this triad contrives to haunt me every day of my life for it was in summer that my generation left school for war, and several dozen that one knew (but strictly speaking did not love, except perhaps for one) were killed, and so never lived to know what I have known—the Beatles, black power, the Administration of Richard Nixon—all this has taken place in a trivial aftertime and has nothing to do with anything that really mattered, with summer and some-one hardly remembered, a youth—not Eric—so abruptly translated from vivid, well-loved (if briefly) flesh to a few scraps of bone and cartilage scattered among the volcanic rocks of Iwo Jima. So much was cruelly lost and one still mourns the past, particularly in darkened movie houses, weeping at bad films, or getting drunk alone while watching the Late Show on television as our summer's war is again refought and one sees some-times what looks to be a familiar face in the battle scenes —is it Jimmy? But the image is promptly replaced and one will never know whether it was he or only a mem-ber of the Screen Actors Guild, now grown old, too.

But in 1948, the war three years behind us, the Ko-rean war not yet upon us—the American empire quies-cent, gorged with conquest—we lived as though it would be forever summer, and did not brood upon our losses. It was enough that Eric Van Damm should say, "Well, come on in," as I started to leave, embarrassed to find him without clothes. Without self-consciousness or coquetry, he continued to polish lenses as I sat awkwardly on the sagging bed while he asked me what I thought of Marietta.

Now Marietta wants to know what I had thought of him. I answer, truthfully, that although I have a sensuous memory of him I do not, strictly speaking, *think* of him. I don't tell her that what I best recall are long legs covered with golden hair. To be candid with Marietta means to be fixed for all time in the distorting aspic of her prose.

"I loved him." Marietta can say that sort of thing in a most winning way; it is only when she writes that she loses.

"Is he still in California?" The last I had heard of Eric he was making documentaries for television.

Marietta gave me a long look, then she said, very carefully, "If you had read *The Heart's Archery*, which I'm sure you got, you would have known that Eric is dead . . ."

Saw the long legs reduced to bone; saw the blue eyes glaze, and fall back into the skull; saw the skull without skin, lips, smile. Yet it is summer in Rome as I write these lines.

"How?"

But Marietta is an artist first, a messenger second. "I've known for some time that you take no interest in my work. Or anything outside yourself . . ."

Some minutes later when she had exhausted herself if not the subject, I learned that Eric had fallen off a roof while filming a riot in Berkeley.

"Such a ridiculous way to die." Marietta was blunt, having no more fear of death than of life.

"Anyway, I have something of his which I want to show you." She opened her handbag and removed a scruffy red notebook of the sort French children use in school, and a manuscript.

"He left these by mistake in Paris, for that sister of his . . ."

That sister of his! Erika had been a perfect feminine version of Eric's own perfect youth. Fantasies of the two of them (they were twins, she dark, he fair) have figured, I am certain, in a thousand erotic dreams for they were rare beings, and quite unknowable. Each made love with the same sort of kind good humor, yet neither seemed entirely present in the act. I looked at the notebook hopefully. Was I about to find out why?

"I was quite upset that summer, as you remember."

I do not but said I did.

"It was understood that he stay in my room at the Hôtel de l'Université until I got back from Turkey. Well, when I came back he had left with what's her name, the bad actress . . . ?"

Memory stirred. "Didn't you use that in your novel, *The Archaic Smile*?"

Marietta looked at me like a child given a present. She was, for an instant, a girl again. "Yes! Yes! Oh, you did read *Smile*! It won the Prix d'Avignon, you know, in French. Yes, I wrote all about Eric and me, and his disappearing, and then running into him years later in Monterey as though nothing had happened. Yes, I wrote it all, just the way it was . . ."

"You never invent, do you?" I could not resist the comment.

"Why should I? The only thing that matters is the life. What *really* happened. You make up everything, don't you?"

"Oh, yes. Everything. Even you."

But she was not listening.

"Now. I want your professional advice. I read somewhere that you were doing the film of *Myra Breckinridge*."

"Not exactly. Someone named Zanuck is doing it. He is very talented. But I am doing a screenplay of *Julian*."

"Strange the way you've always been drawn to history. I hate the past. You're very like Eric, you know, he liked classical history, too. This . . ." She held up the script. ". . . takes place in the third century B.C." I felt a premonitory weariness at the thought of Eric as guide to that lost world.

Then Marietta was all business. She wants to sell the script to a movie producer. With Eric dead, she would be able to keep the money from the sale and buy the Positano villa which, until now, she only rents. "I think I should ask a hundred thousand dollars for it, don't you?"

I tried to explain to her that it was most unlikely that anyone would want to make a film based on a twenty-year-old screenplay by an unknown writer, but Marietta was confident. "That sort of thing is extremely popular now. Look at Fellini and *Satyricon*. The timing couldn't be better. And with you knowing all these film people . . . well, I'm sure you'll find somebody who'll buy it. You are such a friend, really!"

"What is the notebook?"

Marietta frowned. "Very odd. I don't think you'll like it. After all, you're in it. We all are."

"A diary?"

"No. Just . . . well, you'll see. Eric was not what he seemed."

I realized at that moment that I did not want to read either notebook or script. Most people—and all women

9

—are eager to read other people's mail, eavesdrop upon other people's conversations, to find out just what it is that others say of them. I am the opposite. I have no desire to know the worst or for that matter the best, unlike Marietta who reads everything written about her. From Kyoto to Spokane, book reviewers have been astonished to receive long letters from Marietta, analyzing what they have said of her and though no praise has ever been quite sufficient (I compared her once to Katherine Mansfield; she did not speak to me for a year), Marietta is a master of "ensorcelling" those who write book chat for the press, turning to them that legendary Aphrodite face which D. H. Lawrence had on three—no, three and a half—occasions scratched with his bronze fox beard. The reviewer has not been born who can entirely resist the full panoply of such all-conquering charm; as a result, her pen pals now range across the earth and her fame increases with each passing year for, truth to tell, Marietta is an astonishingly good writer of the sacred monster sort and the decades in which she was regarded as something of a joke ("Claire Clairmont without the wit," Cyril Connolly was supposed to have said) made her not only bitter but strong and infinitely cunning in exhibiting both self and work as one until, just as the postwar period became prewar (circa 1965), she was able to enter her kingdom for she is exactly what the times require: a writer who is neither more nor less than what he writes. Entirely lacking in the creative imagination, Marietta Donegal is triumphant, though not as rich as she would like to be.

"I do need money." She rose to go. "Mario is waiting in the Piazza Navona." I have long since stopped asking her to identify for me the Marios and Guidos, the Benjamins and Dereks who are forever waiting a

few streets away, priests of her cult, and with the passing years no doubt well paid for their ministrations at
that high and entirely public altar.

"We're driving down to Positano tomorrow. I'll
come by in the morning, to see what you think."

Dramatically she embraced me on the terrace. Over
her shoulder I could see the two plasterers, morbidly
eager for another glimpse of that ancient dauntless flesh
but to my relief she disappointed them, and allowed me
to lead her inside the apartment, still cool with the
early morning of a fine summer day.

At the front door, Marietta pauses. "Do you believe
in possession?"

"Nine parts of the law?"

"No. Spiritual possession. One person's spirit inhabit-
ing another person's body, mind, personality."

"Marietta, I do not believe in ghosts, astrology, palm-
istry, graphology, John Cage, love or God. I do believe
in the moment, in the pleasures of the flesh, of conversation, of art—at least for the few so minded. I believe . . ."

"What is art?" Marietta is a tough in-fighter, and
knows all the right questions. Unfortunately she is
driven to give wrong answers. She is very effective on
television panel programs.

"If I told you what art was you would turn into a
pillar of salt."

"A pity you never wrote with so much feeling as you
did in *The City and the Pillar*. Of course it was a very
young book but—oh, what a good time we had in New
York that winter! At least I did. But then I've always
been freer than you—and that's all I really wanted for
you, to release your inhibitions, to teach you to *flow*,
to put you on the throne, Dauphin to my Joan."

"You were Joan all right but unfortunately I was

Gilles de Rais." This was halfhearted. As usual, Marietta had managed a series of low blows.

"You are too intellectual, my dear. Too self-absorbed ever to allow yourself to *flow* . . ."

"I'm not a river." I was brisk. "Who was possessed by whom—or what?"

"Eric. Now don't look like that. I'm quite serious. I've always believed that the dead continue to exist. Somehow. Somewhere. And I think that sometimes they even inhabit us, speak through us . . ."

"Have you been getting messages from Eric?"

"No. But last fall in Taos I saw Lawrence, in front of the post office."

"How did he look?"

"Troubled. He was carrying a large cactus in a pot."

"Did he speak?"

"No. He was just there. Briefly. Then he faded. Like a mirage. Like a vision of water in a road on a hot day. Poor Lawrence. How he suffered. Trapped by that dreadful Frieda . . ."

Marietta was drifting off course. "Eric." I tugged her back to the subject.

"You'll see when you read what he's written. *If* he wrote it and not someone else."

"Who else?"

But Marietta enjoys mystery, having none herself. "Someone dead for more than two thousand years."

Depression began. "Not Jesus of Nazareth, a simple carpenter with a lesson for all men?" The golden Eric was capable of dross.

"No. Someone quite different. Anyway, you'll be fascinated. I was. Eric was not the person we thought. Not at all. But the film could be marvelous. Ten percent for you, if you can place it."

Marietta was gone. I sit now on the terrace, beneath

the lemon tree which, each year, produces so many blossoms but never the expected lemon. Just above the tree, a daytime moon, ash white on blue, and circled at this very minute by three Americans, with a flag.

To read, or not? I dread meeting myself in Eric's pages. In a sense, the only purpose of life is the creation of a self and what matters, finally, is the sum total of all one's attempts. By themselves, the early drafts are simply glum reminders that at any given moment in one's youth unripeness was all; the latest draft, for all its flaws, at least has the charm of familiarity; with all those x'ings and interlinear additions it is still somehow *right*, and though the basic text varies little from youth to age, the means of execution shift and change.

Last summer at Sag Harbor, listening to Dwight Mac-Donald talk on and on, entirely happy in his pursuit of thought, I said, "Don't you realize, Dwight, you have nothing to say, only to add?" He stopped short; said he found this a most impressive statement (he has the ability to listen while talking—a rare gift, alas, not mine). Yet what I said of him I really meant to say of myself, of us all. For what is there to *say*, finally, except that pain is bad and pleasure good, life all, death nothing? To these obvious texts, one can only add one's life which is so little, particularly if words are one's only means of telling what was, what is, what ought to be. Marietta commands battalions, divisions, armies (of night and day) of words and yet loses every war. While I am a solitary rifleman behind a tree, waiting to shoot down the pale rider when at last he appears (even as I write this, I hear the earthy drumming of his horse's hooves). But as I wait for him, M.1 at the ready, I know that victory in our private war is already his—structured that way, as the academics say— and all that matters is the accuracy with which one

isolates that pale head, holds it in the gun's sight, and
fires: so death dies and one's life, too. Perhaps it is only
the tree which matters, and the long waiting. In any
case, master of armies or lonely sharpshooter, the
enemy is plain. Eric used film (not words) and fell
while taking pictures from a roof, and all that's left of
him for me as I sit now beneath a lemon tree on the
terrace of a Roman flat is what I am about to read.

THEN

You want to know just what I'm doing and
thinking so I'll start where we left off. You took
the train to Le Havre at eleven and at three o'clock
I went to see that movie producer you think so
awful, well, he is but fascinating and hot for you,
did you know that? "I luff your sister," he has said
to me twice. You should become a movie star. The
work is easy, the money's good but going to bed
with Murray Morris is a high price.

Morris Murray? No. Murray Morris. I'm always
getting the name wrong. Yesterday I called him
Mr. Murray. Then when he said just call me Murray, I called him Mr. Morris. When he changed it
he should've come up with something a bit more
memorable, and less confusing, like Delmore
Schwartz or Plantagenet Cohen.

I think Murray's Polish originally though he
keeps talking about Vienna and how he was a doctor of philosophy before he went to work at UFA
and then Hollywood. Now he's finished with Hollywood "forever, baby" and setting up in Paris to
make "feature-length A-type films of a mature
point of view without the cretinous restrictions of
the studio system in Hollywood where even my
picture *Love at the Finland Station,* in spite of *two*

Academy Award nominations in 1940, was gelded by RKO." The accent is so thick that at first I thought he was referring to Rita Hayworth's *Gilda*, a three-erection film if there ever was one but he meant "gelded."

I don't know why I keep thinking he is flat-ass broke but I do even though the reception people at the Prince de Galles always look pleased whenever we walk by the desk, which must mean he pays his bills since he's been there in a suite for three months, living on room service.

Today was typical. I arrive at three. I knock on the door. No answer. Knock again. Start to go. The door opens a crack. He puts his nose through the crack. It is the largest nose I have ever seen close up. The eyes are small and bright, like a rhinoceros or a wild boar.

"Why are you so early?" He begins each of our sessions with an attempt at putting me on the defensive. I ignore it which really irritates him. I don't even say I'm on time, which is true. "You want me to come back later?"

But Murray pulls me into the room. He is wearing a silk dressing gown, the several hairs on his pointed head rise at various angles. I think what a good shot that would be: those hairs rising like seaweed from smooth sand (a filter light to suggest underwater); then suddenly go to a long shot, and we see it's not seaweed but hair on a head, Murray Morris's head.

In the bedroom, two girls are having at each other on the bed. What am I supposed to do?

Murray grins. "Like schools girls, from the convent, when the nuns are not looking."

I get the range. "You're Father confessor?"

15

Murray has no humor but some wit. "I am the Mother Superior who catches them in the act and paddles them."

Which is what he proceeded to do, all three working from a master script studied the previous day. So far I would say that Murray is a meticulous craftsman in just about everything except film-making.

Although my French isn't good enough to get every nuance of school girl slang mixed with religious admonitions, I could see that the girls had been brilliantly rehearsed. By the time Murray arrived at the grand finale, working the hairbrush rapidly from Buttock One to Buttock Four like a xylophonist, I was ready to come, too. But Murray was not about to share anything except the spectacle which ended when he himself turned red in the face and with a gasp achieved climax beneath, thank God, the silk robe.

Then all three mopped up and the girls left and Murray was now ready to talk business over a glass of sparkling Burgundy. Being young and unimportant, I don't rate champagne. "What I want is to show love on the screen as it has never been shown before."

"Like that?" I indicated the bedroom and the rumpled sheets, the sodden towels, the lingering smell of those excited "school girls."

"Baby, baby." He shook his head at my coarseness. "That is not love, that is . . . that is *play*."

"Well, I'd like to make a playful film."

But for Murray art is one thing, life another and never shall the two coincide if he can help it. Apparently those years at RKO brainwashed him despite the constant companionship and spiritual guidance of Franz Werfel, author of *The Song of Bernadette*, an unreadable writer he likes to quote.

"I want," Murray paused, probing one nostril with a stubby finger on which glittered a diamond ring, eyes half shut as he communed with his muse, Mammon's sister. "I want to make a film of . . . *scope*."

I nodded to show that I, too, was wedded to scope.

"It must be of . . . classical proportions like Aeschylus."

Murray has probably read Aeschylus or at least he has taken the trouble to read a good synopsis of the *Oresteia*. He is full of cultural surprises.

"Yet . . ." He paused dramatically, unplugging his nose. "This film must speak to the people *now*, to the housewife in Pomona, to the garage attendant in Newark, to the . . . the . . ."

"The little people?"

Murray nodded, pleased. Jesus, what a whore I am! And I enjoy it, I really do, but then you always said I had no character, that I take on the personality of the person I'm with which makes it pretty odd when we're together, since we are the same: two sponges—or are you different? I am never certain.

"Eric. I. have. faith. in. you." That's the way he said it, gravely, carefully, as though testifying in court, something he has probably done quite a bit of. "Your film I loved. The prize you won at Cannes should've given you the world market but you did not get it, and do you know why?"

"Well, it was just a documentary, about dancers . . ."

"You did not get a world market because you

did not have Murray Morris, Murray Morris who from the first inception of a script can guide your pen. Oh, I'm no writer!" He laughed to show that if he wanted to he could create *The Magic Mountain* with one hand while paddling a convent of nuns with the other.

"I don't pretend to be able to write or direct. *But!* I do know talent, quality. It was I, Murray Morris, who found in this obscure German magazine the short story on which I based *Love at the Finland Station* with its two Academy Award nominations. It was Murray Morris who mixed the ingredients." He stirred a great invisible salad for my benefit. I tried to look hungry. "And that is my function, my dream, to make films of scope with a negative cost of no more than two hundred thousand five while holding below the line costs in Europe to one hundred five, and not a penny more."

No, I don't know any more about the intricacies of the movie business than you do but he does sound plausible, and though it is madness to trust him, I've got nothing to lose. After all, he is giving me a chance to write an honest-to-God film and— maybe—direct, though I can't believe that will come true.

"It is because of this respect I have for your film that I want to work with you closely, teaching you everything I know, like a mediaeval master and his . . . acolyte?"

"Apprentice."

"Apprentice." He patted the telephone. "Do you know who I have a call in to at this very moment?"

I looked at the telephone as though it might speak a holy name. But it was Murray who spoke the name, voice hushed, eyes suddenly watering. "Garbo!"

We were both so moved that for a long moment we could do nothing but stare at the telephone which he continued to stroke as though it was indeed the actual container of that famous legend. Then Murray leaned forward and whispered in my ear, so that the telephone might not overhear, "*She will return to the cinema for Murray Morris.*"

"What sort of role?"

Murray was now on his feet. "The thing that struck me about you, baby, is not only your fine— if unappreciated by the public—film but your cultural background which so few Americans have, if I may say so. You were a classical scholar at Harvard . . ."

"Not really. Actually it was at prep school that . . ."

"You know Greek . . ."

"Not any more . . ."

"Don't run yourself down, baby. I want to do a film to be made on location in Greece where I have this wonderful relationship with Kimon Veloudious."

"Who?"

He looked at me with pity for my ignorant youth. "The Minister of Culture, and a fine poet. We were at the university together in Prague." This was new. Usually he spoke only of the university of Vienna. Obviously Murray was a real wandering scholar, an UFA goliard.

"They want me to make a major film in Athens, using the army if we want, the countryside, the beautiful vistas like the Parthenon at dusk. 'Maid of Athens, ere we part, give me back . . .' "

"Byron!" I said. "A wonderful subject."

Hurt at being interrupted, he said, "You jump too fast on conclusions. I've noticed this before."

True to my policy, I did not acknowledge his offensive. Instead I continued to play the perfect sixth former that I never was but can on occasion appear to be.

"No. Something more important than Byron. Something both more usual and more unusual. A story of two sisters who are rivals in everything. One marries a bona fide king. The other marries the Great King of Persia. They torment each other, betray each other, yet . . . *yet* they love each other for they know that the only person in the world who really understands them are they." When excited, he has trouble with pronouns.

"Is there a plot?"

"Is there a plot? *Is there a plot?* Baby, there is the plot!" Murray took a folder from the desk. On the cover was written "The Two Sisters of Ephesus, a treatment by Murray Morris and Clyde R. Bannister Jr." Just under the title three perfect coffee rings linked themselves like the ancient symbol of Olympus.

"Who is Clyde R. Bannister Jr?"

"A fink. Don't worry. I have a signed release from him that the property is mine. You will read it overnight. You will study it. You will love it, as I do. Then we shall put our heads together and we shall create a film that will make the world gasp, a story of scope, of love and hate, of religious passion, of ecstasy and, yes . . . there will be erotic scenes but all done in perfect taste. Do you realize that no Murray Morris picture has ever failed to get the Seal? Yet every Murray Morris film has

broken new ground. Remember the use of the word
urning in *Love at the Finland Station?* It was Murray Morris who first brought that word to the
screen, and in perfect taste, evolving naturally out
of the context as will all our scenes of pagan sensuality run riot beneath the blazing skies of Greece
where Sappho sang and burned, where . . ."

"Which part is for Garbo?"

"Fuck Garbo! We are making a screenplay.
When it's finished, she should be so lucky as to be
considered after *Two Faced Woman,* that flop
where she played twin sisters, come to think of
it. She must never play a sister again. Never!"

Murray pounced on the telephone. "Cancel the
call to Greta Garbo. Merci." He hung up. "I feel
like a bum. She has looked forward so long to
working with me but . . . well, that's show business."

Murray led me to the door, heavy arm about my
shoulder. "Same time tomorrow." He kissed me full
on the lips. "And, baby, don't be late like you were
today."

NOW

What do I think of Eric now?

I stare off at the dome of Sant' Agnese just over the
trellis at the terrace's edge and think it not unlike the
head of Murray Morris whom I last saw some months
ago, entering the Baur au Lac hotel at Zurich, clutching a large black briefcase. Since 1948, he has made and
lost several fortunes. Currently he is said to be "in
trouble." As usual, he greeted me with the cry, "We
must work together, baby!" He held the black briefcase close to his stomach as though afraid I might
somehow get it away from him as he, no doubt, had

wrested its contents from the Bureau of Internal Revenue.

"I have a property you would love, for Taylor and Burton. Come to my suite at five, I have a call in to Elizabeth—she loves your work, you know—and I'm sure she and I together will be able to persuade Richard. You know how he is but don't worry, I will fix it."

As Murray started toward the lift, I asked, mischievously, "What are you doing in Zurich?"

Without turning around, he said, "I am here to be skiing." The month was August. I am fond of Murray. He will lie even when it is inconvenient, the sign of the true artist.

I wish I had asked him about Eric but then I had not thought of Eric in months—years? Memory is fitful at best. People come and go at random in the swift uncertain circuits of the brain, and with each year one loses more and more names and faces while even sexual encounters tend to blur one into another (what exactly happened that night in a Seattle suburb before I went overseas from Fort Lewis?).

Yet now that I deliberately put my mind to it, I can *see* Eric as he was, or at least as he was that day in the Hôtel de l'Université, taking apart the camera. I suddenly recall, as I write these words, that his two front teeth were chipped, not the most romantic memory of that Beatrice to my Dante—or perhaps Tadzio is the better analogy.

A moment of panic. What *did* happen? Who was he, and did I ever really know him? So far the red notebook reveals someone I never met. A tough, worldly young man with a will to prevail and, as I suspected then, a special relationship with his sister. . . . That does it! For the first time in years I have used without irony the word "relationship." An hour with Marietta and I am a creature of the Forties again when hardly a paragraph was spoken or written without that terrible jargon word.

The Eric I knew—or thought I knew and still recall from time to time like the phrase in *Don Carlos* which recurs so hauntingly at each encounter between doomed prince and revolutionary friend—that Eric was a golden solitary, intent upon his art, totally and seriously absorbed by film long before the *Cahiers du Cinéma* was dreamed of. He could never have known Murray Morris. Yet he did. And it is chillingly plain that I have allowed that unexpected sentimentalist, my memory, to make Eric something he never was or—alarming thought—chose even at the time to mythologize him.

I am shaken. Do I never get the point to those I—the word could be "love" though I never use it? Yet am I not always in my careful (or so I think) self-scrutiny always quick to determine what is lust and what is sympathy? The first is common; the second rare. The two together not possible except by an act of the imagination. For me the two did coincide at a particular point in time on a hot summer day in a Paris hotel room, or so I thought until now when it seems that my imagination may have created something which did not, in fact, exist. But then none of us exists except in terms of others and so with each person not only a different performance but a different self. Later, when alone, as images come and go, constantly changing, we begin to feel, and then invent. Love affairs can only take place after the act, in memory, at a decent remove from urgent flesh and that colliding of masks which seldom does more than meliorate the fact of two hostile and alien—yet so similar—wills.

The Eric of the notebook is someone I never knew; also, reading him, I get no sense of the Paris of my youth. Have I invented that too?

What will he say of me? Or Erika? I detest Marietta for having done this to me. But it is too late to stop now. I go on reading as the past devours the present.

THEN

You remember *The Last Days of Pompeii* which we thought so wonderful when we were kids and then saw again last year in the Village and thought so awful? Well, that is what Murray and Clyde R. Bannister Jr have done in their treatment, a sort of Brown Derby version of the past. Fearing plagiarism, Murray won't let the treatment out of his hands for more than a few hours at a time; otherwise, I'd send you a copy.

I did show it to V. and he said it was sure to be successful since everything in it is false: history, psychology, etc.

NOW

I have no memory of ever reading such a treatment. He calls me V. What am I to make of that?

THEN

But I told him that to have the chance of making a real movie at age twenty-three is the important thing. Tennessee Williams agrees with me. He and V. are on the same floor as I am, with Williams in the room you used to have. Williams is not at all what you might expect the most successful playwright since Shakespeare—well, O'Neill—would be like. He has a funny laugh, heh-heh-heh, and a habit of biting his knuckles in order to make them

24

crack. Last night he gave a party in the hotel with a lot of French actors and actresses who want to be in Cocteau's version of *A Streetcar Named Desire*—and think what a mess that will be in this country! Anyway Sartre was supposed to come but instead sat all alone down the street in the bar of the Pont Royal and when one of the guests who knows him went to fetch him, refused to come. Very French. Williams was highly pissed off.

"I have always depended upon the kindness of strangers." Why is that such a powerful line? It keeps going through my head. Maybe because it's strangers I like in bed. There's only one person not a stranger I could ever bear for long.

NOW

As for Sartre, twenty years later he is still upon the scene. I saw him last night with de Beauvoir at Il Buco. I was amused to note that neither mandarin had much to say to the other. They were like an old married couple. *"Les mots sont versés, il faut les boire."*

THEN

Certainly not Marietta. You were right about her. She *is* an egomaniac but also very touching, and sexy—at least I find her so, particularly when she is acting out Daudet's *Sappho,* making me feel young and raw and selfish (all things that I am but, hopefully, more) and talks about her famous lovers in order to make me feel grateful for having qualified for inclusion in such a distinguished anthology. Yet she is marvelous in the sack, does X and Y, and, as for Z, better than you know who!

NOW

I don't think anyone ever suspected that brother and

sister discussed with one another what they did in bed. But why not? They were twins. The same?

THEN

Unfortunately, as you know, I can only stay interested just so long in somebody and then their body starts to depress me. The novelty's gone and with it all desire. I'd like a harem, with a thousand inmates.

Meanwhile I'm just a figure in Marietta's harem. Which I don't like. Luckily, she's gone to Turkey to write something for *Colliers* and won't be on the scene until fall by which time I hope we're shooting the film and I'm miles away from her, both physically and financially. She lent me twelve hundred dollars just before she left and that should get me through the summer, though I'm counting on Murray to come through. At the moment I'm working on what is called in the trade "speculation" or "spec" for short, and with Murray it's pretty short.

I told Murray I thought the treatment was swell. He was pleased. "Baby, what do you think of Robert Taylor for Herostratus?"

"Interesting."

"I can get him for peanuts. We'll talk to him together, on the phone, to get his thinking on the part."

Wanting to be impressive, I'm afraid I lied and got into trouble. I said that Tennessee Williams had advised me to do the script. This was true. However, I didn't tell him that Williams had been unable to read the treatment.

I'd overplayed my hand. Murray sprang to his feet, like a rhinoceros at the sight of whatever it is that arouses a rhinoceros, another rhinoceros, I suppose. "You know my old friend Tennessee? He is here?"

Fortunately I got the range. I lied quickly. "Yes, but he left this morning for London."

With hurt wonder: "He was here, and never called Murray Morris, Murray Morris who offered him his first screenplay that he turned down to write, can you *believe* it? *Marriage Is a Private Affair,* which bombed, with Lana Turner at Metro."

"I don't think he's doing movies anymore."

"He could do this one. Where is he staying in London?"

I said I didn't know, said Williams had turned down ten million dollars or something for a screenplay, and got myself back on the job.

Moodily, Murray picked at the remains of his lunch; as usual, I sat while he ate. Only once has he ever acknowledged I might be hungry when he held out a plate of rolls and said, "Have some breads." Occasionally his plurals betray national origin. He looked relieved when I said no.

Then: "O.K., baby. Do you want to take a crack at it?"

I was not sure at what I was to take a crack.

"The screenplay. Start in."

"Yes. Yes, I would. Very much. But about the— well, the money . . ."

"With Murray Morris, money is unimportant." He thrust one of the breads into his mouth and continued to talk while chewing. "*Participation* is what matters in these deals, not the money up front. I wouldn't insult you with a salary. You're not some Screenwriters Guild hack, baby, you are

27

an artist, and more than that, you are my partner, share and share alike. . . ."

Anyway, with my gift for business inherited from our father (remember when he bought those orange groves in Florida that were half a mile out to sea, *under* the sea?), I'm to get a thousand dollars once the screenplay is finished, and a percentage which he carefully wrote out for me on a piece of paper in terms I can't understand—what is one third of one percent of the profits after negative cost has been regained one and a half times? And then he forgot to sign it. Well, I can always keep the script until I'm paid. Now I must write it.

In a funny way, there *is* something in the story even though Murray is intent on homogenizing everything in order to appeal to the housewife in Schenectady. Two sisters battling one another from birth is as good a theme as any to demonstrate everybody's desire to get what he wants which, in classic times at least, was often best expressed through women. After all, it was Medea, not Jason, who killed the children.

The two sisters have a brother Herostratus. I want to tell the story through him—after all, he is the only one still remembered—but Murray wants to concentrate on the girls, show them growing up in Ephesus . . . and what in Christ's name did *that* look like in the third century B.C.? I'm trying to get hold of one of the prewar Baedekers for a description.

Apparently, the ruins of Ephesus are now in Turkey, on the sea, in what used to be Asia Minor. It was a Greek city, occupied by Persians at the time our story begins. I love that phrase: it spreads the blame so conveniently. As our story begins, a

28

beautiful young girl is seen cording wool at a window. Dark-haired, pert-nosed she resembles Ava Gardner (this means Miss Gardner will be the first actress offered the part. When she turns it down, Ida Lupino's name will be substituted. I'm learning a lot from Murray).

But what is Ephesus to me? St. Paul writing one of his disagreeable memoranda to its citizens. And the Temple of Diana, the greatest temple of the ancient world which wasn't really dedicated to the Diana we know, that cool dyke with the bow and arrows, but to a far more ancient goddess—the original mother of the earth, usually shown with a small child just like Mary and Jesus.

In fact, our own gallant Mary is the same great mother goddess adapting herself slyly to the new nonsense. Proof: according to the Church, Mary withdrew to Ephesus (after the unpleasantness at Golgotha) and there lived quietly in a bungalow until wafted to heaven by Pius XII and our own Mother Spellman. Since the first century there has been an important shrine to Mary at Ephesus just as for twelve hundred years before that there was a temple to her first incarnation, sometimes known as Diana.

But already Murray wants to be anachronistic. In 356 B.C. (when our girls are in their prime), the goddess Diana was depicted rather like Mary with Jesus. Not until the next century was she shown as a kind of monster-lady covered with tits from chin to crotch. Unfortunately, Murray loves the monster-lady. "Just think, baby, we can actually *show* this statue on the screen and there's not a thing the Johnston office can do because it's historical!"

"But it's not historical. The tits weren't standard equipment at the time of our story, etc." He just looks hurt whenever I tell him this. So the opening shot is sure to be that statue with its one hundred (count them) breasts.

I sometimes wonder if that is why Murray was first drawn to the story. He is a labyrinth of false clues and pretentious passageways, all leading toward something obvious like the cock or the cunt. I can't understand why he has not been more successful in Hollywood. I suppose it's knowing too many of those *Kaffeeklatsch Mitteleuropa* intellectuals like Franz Werfel. They've prevented Murray from having the courage of his own vulgarity.

So I took a crack at the script. I locked myself into the room, hunched over the broken Corona (the *e* is now gone. I use an *x*. It drives Murray wild), and wrote the script in seven days. Then the troubles began.

NOW

I can understand why. I've read the script which Marietta wants me to sell, and it is impossible by any standard. A perfect example of what happens when two people who have not the slightest understanding of one another decide to work together on a subject neither has any real feeling for. The result is always painful—though sometimes enormously successful with the public. Unfortunately for Marietta there is no longer a public which would accept *The Two Sisters of Ephesus first revised screenplay (24-8-48) by Eric Van Damm and Murray Morris based on an original treatment by Clyde R. Bannister Jr and Murray Morris* (Murray was already horning in on the credits, an old trick of his). Not only were the two authors at cross purposes but the subject itself never came into focus. I think I know why. Eric was interested in Herostratus. Murray was interested in the possibility of tempting Lana Turner and Ava Gardner, the two reigning queens of the box office, to play Artemisa and Helena, the eponymous sisters. Knowing Murray's ability to get his way, I was not surprised to read scene after scene of Artemisa or Helena relaxing in the bath surrounded by beautiful ladies-in-waiting, diaphanous gowns clinging to their nubile forms, as the late W. C. Fields used to say. There was even a paddling scene that had the unmistakable Murray Morris stamp. It is the only scene in which either of the authors appears to be entirely committed to what he is writing. The rest is *Kitsch* without sincerity which means, to continue in low German, *Dreck*.

THEN

Half asleep, I opened the door to my room the morning after I gave Murray the script and there he was, wearing a beret, a yellow silk ascot, a blue blazer, and carrying the script under his arm. He looked like an anti-Semitic cartoon (Berlin '33).

Luckily I was alone. Since you left I've taken in a big way to the continental habit of *cinq à sept*. For one thing, as you know, I like light and can think of nothing more marvelous than to lie on that great broken-backed bed in the full sunlight as I explore and probe a new body—oh, it is a lovely custom, no doubt of that, and makes for perfect evenings, free for talk and food, no restless wondering whether or not I'm going to make out and, if I happen to, find myself faced with spending the whole night with someone I've never met before and don't really want to know. I like sex better than people, as Marietta keeps telling me. She's right of course. But what can I do?

"So this is where the young genius lives!" Murray was all smiles, tiny pig eyes twinkling. I knew then that we were in for a major row. Normally, he is disagreeable when we meet but then with the breaking of the breads, we become chummy. This was obviously going to be the breaking of the asses. He examined my camera as though he knew how it worked, getting fingerprints all over the lens.

"You know, Eric, how many times I've told you how much I love this film of yours at Cannes." As much as I like praise, I've come to dread Murray's mention of the film; it is always the first move in an offensive action.

"I don't agree with those who say it was just a fluke." This was obviously going to be Hiroshima-time. A-bomb 1: At twenty-three I'm washed up. A-bomb 2: Flash in the pan. Well, better to have flashed in the pan than never to have flashed at all.

"Murray." I have adopted the Hollywood habit (or is it Jewish? or both?) of addressing him by name just as he invariably calls me Eric—or "baby"—whenever he begins a sentence. I've noticed that most Hollywood scripts are written in the same way. "Marcia, I want you to know something." "What, Bruce, do you want me to know?"

"Murray, everything in that script is what you wanted." I took the offensive, told him that what I had done was exactly what he had wanted me to do, and the result was *his* not my doing.

Then, very thoughtfully, Murray screamed—a high piercing shriek such as Tarzan was wont to use when summoning Tantor, his pachyderm pal.

The hotel's clientele must have been chilled with terror at the sound.

"What are you doing to me, I ask you?" That was the beginning of what was an hour of abuse. Boiled down: too much Herostratus. Not enough sisters. More sex. But not the kind I was writing.

"We can't show them in bed, baby, you know the code. You must *suggest.* Be subtle. At bedtime we see two pillows instead of the one we saw in the A.M."

"They didn't use pillows."

"So who knows that? Some college professor?" The friend of Franz Werfel unexpectedly revealed scorn for the high culture which had sustained him for so long in the vulgar marketplace.

"Be suggestive. Teasing. And more tits. Remember the goddess. This is really about her. She is the emblem, the symbol of what we are doing. The archetypal figure of woman, awesome, maternal, the womb and the grave." He switched just in time to his ancient culture and gave me a dissertation on Woman, with random references to Sappho, Dido, Messalina and Joan of Arc, four ladies who shared but two things in common, their sex and the fact that Murray had remembered their names.

"And who cares about this Herostratus? This mavin? He's just a link."

"But you can't tell two stories."

"Eric, there are no laws," said the lawgiver.

"Why not use Herostratus as a narrator. Then we can shift from one sister to the other, getting to know each through his eyes, bringing them all together at the end, at the temple."

A long moment while Murray shut his eyes,

visualized the entire film, beginning with a blast of trumpets from Max Steiner as "Murray Morris Presents" flashes on the screen and ending with the temple in flames, the goddess crumbling to fiery ash, as Lana and Ava weep softly.

"I like it, baby. But why—*why* didn't you do it that way first? Why do you torture me like this. Make me raise my voice." He indicated the walls of the room. "People might have overheard us and asked themselves where is the *esprit de corps* of these two partners?"

So I'm off again. But this time I'm writing it first as a treatment, as if Herostratus was telling the story. I'm doing the first draft long hand in this notebook so you'll be able to get the full, fresh, no doubt God-awful impression of the thing. It's going to be very cinematic. Not much dialogue. Just pictures. *Action*.

Incidentally, your letter about Benson alarmed me a little. Wanting to escape the family is one thing, and understandable, but to marry a man so much older before you've really had time to look around is crazy. I know his virtues. I also know your faults. Will you complement one another? Or tear each other apart? You've had no emotional life except what we've known together and that is hardly a preparation for marriage.

I'm glad Benson is willing to allow you complete freedom in your private life but at the same time he makes me deeply suspicious. What *quid* does he want for that *quo*? Nothing is ever given, only traded, as Murray so wisely says when he is about to steal something. Anyway, don't do anything impulsive. Try to get on with the family, even if it means an entire summer at Southampton. They're awful but a protection.

I'm surprised that you are impressed by the fact that Benson is president of an electronics firm. At forty-seven a man can't avoid being president of something unless of course he has talent. I want a fuller report on what he is like in bed. And find out why his first wife left him.

NOW

What a pair! And how unexpected.

I first saw them at the Café de Flore in the summer of 1948. They were seated side by side at the center of the first row of sidewalk tables, quite outshining Sartre and de Beauvoir who were holding court nearby. Obviously the sight of two so splendidly *untouched* (or so they seemed) Americans was most exciting for the French who were in those days somewhat more grubby and irritable than is usual even for that untidy race.

How did they actually look? Fair hair, dark hair, similar features. No, that is too general. Try again. Think of clothes. Like the rest of us, Eric wore the remains of his army uniform, khaki trousers and shirt (for ten years I wore my army belt until the webbing snapped) while Erika wore—well, I have no idea what anyone wears unless it is in some way vivid like the see-through dress I encountered last night at a Roman party, the girl's breasts plain beneath pink and white striped gauze. All agreed the left was perfect; the right flawed.

In any case, Erika was as beautiful as Eric and where-ever they went together, they reigned. Particularly at the Hôtel de l'Université where they shared two rooms until Marietta arrived to continue her "relationship" with me. As I was otherwise engaged, she moved in with Eric, and Erika took the room next to mine on the floor above.

Last year when I visited Paris I was happy to see that the Hôtel de l'Université has reappeared. For a long time it was an office building and no matter how carefully I prowled the quarter, like Le Grand Meaulnes, I could not recall which of the row of eighteenth century buildings opposite the Ministry of Finance was the scene of my youth.

Now things look very much the way they were but of course they are not. For one thing youth is gone. Worse, the Paternaults who ran the hotel are gone. Madame was a splendid cook, and thoughtful. "Mr. Weeks," she said one morning to an Iowan aesthete, "I sometimes notice a curious smell coming from your room. Today we expect the police. If there is anything you would like me to hide, I will." Without a word, Weeks gave her his pipe and cache of opium and so was not caught in the great drug roundup of 1948.

There was also a good deal of sexual traffic that summer. The stairs creaked at all hours as lovers came and went, moving from room to room, floor to floor, sometimes, in the case of at least one energetic girl (now a leading matron in San Antonio), making several errands of mercy in a single night.

But Erika was enigmatic. As far as I know, she went to bed with no one except a young American actor who —or so she told Eric who told Marietta who told me— was infantile in bed. Marietta used this particular episode to good advantage in one of her privately printed novels (hard to believe that in those days she was forced to be her own publisher), excoriating not, as was fashionable then, that national villain the American mom, but the men who so loved themselves that they could not properly appreciate the truly, deeply feminine, that is to say, Marietta. Long before Leslie Fiedler began to monitor Huck Finn's raft, Marietta was confident that all American men were basically homosexual and so incapable of appreciating Woman, the first principle of the universe. Nevertheless, she refused to admit defeat; and at regular intervals, like a goddess, she would descend from her heart-shaped machine and ensorcel men into worshipping her, or at least going to bed with her. Eric took to her in much the same way I had.

My own friendship with Eric was tentative due to shyness on both sides for we were the same age which is as great a barrier to friendship among the young as it is an invitation to comity among the old. Also, I was notorious that summer for my third novel, written at twenty-one, was not only a best seller but a source of rage to many, not all writers. As a result, Eric regarded me warily, and with some reason.

Nevertheless, despite all that was not said—and done —brother, sister and I spent many evenings together, usually ending up at the *Boeuf sur le Toit* whose long decline had even then begun, unknown to us, as we joined the other young Americans who came to the Rue du Colisée, hoping that by simply being at the *Boeuf* they would become part of the prewar Paris of Picasso, Cocteau, Milhaud, none aware that this was a new time, and that *we* were that time as we sat and drank and talked of—what? Ourselves, I suppose, as the young must, and of course Literature (my subject: not since Hemingway was there a young writer so intent on dominance!), Film (Eric's subject: he was one of the first to take seriously the commercial film on which we had all been raised) and Erika. For us she was a subject of constant interest though she never pressed (unlike Marietta), never demanded equal time no matter at what great length Eric and I declared our ambitions and defended our accomplishments.

Needless to say, I was the most defensive, having most to defend. The book of mine which had been such a success that year had been thought to be artless autobiography. No one seemed aware that its art was to *seem* true and artless and that it was, in fact, a work of the imagination, and therefore a rare thing in our letters. Since then I've accepted the fact that my countrymen are literal to the point of—the hand pauses on the page. What shall I say of the country I was born in? Well . . .

For a long time it was hoped that as the civilization whose absence drove Henry James to Europe came slowly to be born in America, the diversity of life might yet be understood and so make possible interesting art. But it was not to be. Civilization has not taken hold even in our alabaster cities. Rather the opposite, for violence is now the order of the day as we produce our crude artifacts and call them art, all the while dreaming those simple lurid dreams which precede, traditionally, a time of fire: so much is ending that was good, so much continuing that was bad.

As for literature—how feeble the word itself sounds in an age of Rock and bright murder—it has no relevance to the young who were brought up on television and movies, and though they are doubtless happier for that whole experience, they are also quite unable to comprehend the *doubleness* of things, the unexpected paradox, the sense of yes-no without which there can be no true intelligence, no means, in fact, of examining life as opposed to letting it wash over one.

Without history, without art, with a memory that begins with each morning's waking and ends with the night's sleep, they are able to achieve a numbness far

more comforting to the spirit than the always dangerous and sometimes fatal exploration of self and world
which was the aim of our old culture, now discarded.

Discarded? Never known.

Last year, the day after the notorious Democratic
Convention in Chicago, the New Party was born (soon
to die) and I was one of its founders. Several hundred
bright young dissidents, appalled by the police riot and
the collapse of Eugene McCarthy, met in a university
auditorium.

At first I was startled by the incoherence of the
speeches but then in the warm mood of our common
cause, I decided that this was the result of shock; and
we were all of us more or less stunned by the bad days
we had been living through.

When it came my turn to speak, I described a meeting I had had that morning with Senator McCarthy.
He had told me that he would not run for President on
our ticket because he thought he would be of more use
supporting good Senatorial candidates. "After all," he
had said wanly, "it was the Roman Senate that saved
Rome." I respected this even though I had felt obliged
to point out that "it wasn't the Senate but the Capito-
line geese that saved Rome."

I usually have some sense of audience. But this time
I had walked into a wall. Those faces which were not
simply bewildered were hostile: what's all this crazy
shit about *geese?* I realized too late that they have in
common no history at all. "The only thing we have to
fear is fear itself" would have been just as puzzling to
the *Now* Generation . . . which is already *then* for as
I write, 1968 is slipping into that limbo where dinosaurs
and Charlemagne, dodoes and LBJ together consort in
nameless darkness.

Trying to recall, after twenty years, what it was we

talked about so late into the night, I suddenly recall that politics was seldom mentioned. After all, Fascism had just been vanquished for all time while Communism was as remote as the Soviet Union, and about as appealing. Eric and I were both too young to have been attracted to the Party the way so many of our older friends had been before the war. As for domestic politics, the summer's choice between Dewey and Truman seemed to be no choice at all.

The only political discussion that I can remember from those days was with Tennessee. It occurred shortly before the Italian elections in which the Communists were expected to win. "The Russians," Tennessee announced most uncharacteristically, "are not a predatory people. I don't know why there is all this fuss about 'international Communism.'"

I disagreed. "They've always been imperialists, just like us."

"That's not true. Just name one country Russia has tried to take over? I mean recently."

"Latvia, Lithuania and Estonia," I began . . .

"And what," asked Tennessee, "are they?"

It is his charm, and genius, to be his own world in which forever turn in hieratic attitudes mother, sister, father, self, a world in no way connected with the one of newspapers and, perhaps for that reason, more durable than our furious quotidian.

I thought of Tennessee early this spring when I checked into a hotel at Amalfi where we had stayed twenty years ago. Now I was alone, making a screenplay for old time's sake of his latest play which I had thought very bad when I saw it but then, after some study, found parts were marvelous, and laughed aloud, hearing, as I read, the wry cadence of his voice, heard our old laughter in the courtyard of the hotel (where

Ibsen wrote *Ghosts*), and marveled to myself that so many years later I would be adapting him in a place we had once stayed before time had played its usual jokes, made him a bit mad and, for me at least, remote, made me . . . the same.

Tennessee traveled with but one book, a handsomely bound (blue-stamped white leather) edition of the poems of Hart Crane. Only now do I begin to fathom those sea-kept fabulous shadows.

THEN
Historical Background to "The Two Sisters of Ephesus."

This is just a reminder for us, Murray, and for anyone who reads the treatment cold. Actually everything that we need to know as far as the film goes we'll see right on the screen and there won't be all this dotting of *I's*. But for ourselves we should know—but not necessarily use or even be faithful to—the following:

It is the summer of 356 B.C. The Persian empire extends from the Tigris and Euphrates to the borders of Macedonia whose king is Philip, soon to be the father of Alexander the Great. The Macedonians are the first power in Greece and a threat to the Persians who for a generation have been engaged in civil war, particularly in Asia Minor where the troublesome Greek-inhabited cities (among them Ephesus) seldom lose an opportunity to revolt.

Shortly before our story begins, the Great King Artaxerxes II Mnemon has managed to subdue the cities. Then, at seventy, he dies, leaving the throne to a most efficient and ruthless son Artaxerxes III Ochus (I don't know what we should do about

41

these names—for now let's call them Mnemon and
Ochus). Together with the eunuch Bagoas (perfect
part for Francis L. Sullivan or Sydney Green-
street), Ochus methodically suppresses all resis-
tance to his regime. This includes a deal with Maussollus of Halicarnassus, which allows Maussollus
to keep the kingdom of Caria which he assembled
during the civil wars, on condition that Maussollus
acknowledge Ochus as his overlord, and accept
demotion to satrap. Maussollus agrees, despite the
objections of his ambitious wife Artemisa, one of
our two sisters. The other is Helena, a wife of the
late Great King Mnemon. I think, all in all, to avoid
confusing the audience, we had better call the
Great King of Persia the Emperor, and Maussollus
King. This makes our girls Empress and Queen
respectively.

The sisters are daughters of Lagus, a distinguished but not wealthy Greek patrician of Ephesus. In 356 Helena is twenty-four years old with
a three-year-old son by the Emperor. Artemisa is
twenty-eight, and childless. Their half brother is
Herostratus (the hero in my first version but now
only the narrator—don't worry!), a revolutionary
and poet. Incidentally, I've moved Maussollus's
death to the summer of 356, three years before it
actually occurred. You'll see why.

Herostratus in Prison.
As a matter of suspense, he should appear to be in
limbo. A man of thirty, clean-shaven in the Greek
style rather than bearded like the Persians. If you
like, he can be handsome. I don't think it makes
much difference as long as the actor who plays
him has the ability to look, from time to time, as

42

if he is actually thinking. This rules out all the youngish American actors, including Brando and your friend Robert Taylor. Perhaps you should go English and take someone like Olivier or Mason.

HEROSTRATUS

I begin, as I end. The fire has done its work, and I am happy, and shall be happy and leave nothing that I care about. For what is Ephesus now but a tomb for my old self? And though I still bear this envelope of flesh, still see, hear, feel, I am not what I was before the fire burned away my mortality and left me free in eternity. Oh, Helena! What is an empress to a god?

The Gates of Ephesus.
A company of Persian horsemen escort a litter toward the city gates where a delegation waits, headed by Pharnabazus, the Satrap of Ephesus; he stands somewhat apart from the others, eyes shut against the glare. On one cheek a birthmark like a purple bat with wings half-furled.
The others: Lagus is large and soft-fleshed, food his principal interest and slow executioner. His wife Arsinoë is small, with a dark sharp face. By virtue of her daughters' marriages she is now the first of the Greek ladies of Ephesus. Yet even when she smiles, she appears to frown; worried perhaps that it is all a dream, that she never married Lagus, never gave birth to a Persian Empress and a Carian Queen, that she is still a merchant's daughter trying to trap Lagus into marrying her.
Herostratus stands beside his father Lagus and his stepmother Arsinoë. With them is Demetrius, the high priest of Diana; a gray man with a beautiful voice which he deliberately pitches so low that his listeners are forced to incline toward him as he speaks. At the moment he is whispering to Lysander, a round-faced historian with a gift for polemic which is always at the service of the sisters;

in fact, so devoted is he to the family that Herostratus once called him the third daughter of Lagus.

HEROSTRATUS'S VOICE

Did you know that the day you returned from Susa, of all those present I alone was happy to see you?

The litter stops. Helena draws back the curtains. Dark-haired, pale-faced, dressed all in white, she looks slowly from face to face, without expression, as though nothing on earth could ever again give her either pleasure or pain. The Satrap Pharnabazus walks toward her. Stops. Raises his arm in hieratic attitude and roars, as if to a crowd.

PHARNABAZUS

Helena, wife to the late Emperor Mnemon, I welcome you to Ephesus in the name of our beloved Emperor Ochus, brother to the sun and moon, may he live a thousand years!

Helena murmurs something that no one can hear and then, grasping the arm of Pharnabazus, she steps down from the litter. Lagus is the first to go to her. They embrace; then Arsinoë takes Helena in her arms.

ARSINOË

Where is the child?

Helena frowns. Predictably, Arsinoë has betrayed interest: the son of an emperor is more important than his widow. Having created, launched and lost her famous daughters, it is now Arsinoë's instinct (she has no conscious mind) to turn to the next generation, to her grandson.
But Helena is a shrewd tactician in the family's wars. Instead of answering her mother, she motions to Herostratus to approach and, as he does, with beautiful deliberateness, Helena smiles. As Herostratus kisses her cheek, Helena whispers in his ear, voice unexpectedly harsh and urgent.

HELENA

Protect me! There is no one else.

The House of Lagus.
It is night. Torches flare in the first and second courtyards. Greeks and Persians mingle. Music plays. Helena sits on a marble throne in the second of the two courts, gravely receiving guests. At her side stands Lysander, carefully repeating the names of those who wish to be presented as if dictating one of his histories to a more than usually slow-witted secretary.

HEROSTRATUS'S VOICE

I was glad that you turned to me. I was glad that you knew I was the only one you could depend on, no matter what happened.

Herostratus stands in the passageway between the two courts, watching Helena as she speaks now to the High Priest Demetrius. Pharnabazus joins him.

PHARNABAZUS

You must tell your sister that she may not use the title empress.

HEROSTRATUS

Does she use it?

PHARNABAZUS

Constantly.

HEROSTRATUS

But why not? After all she was the Emperor's wife.

Pharnabazus is pedantic.

PHARNABAZUS

She was one of twenty wives, and at the end she was not his principal wife, as you know and as she knows.

HEROSTRATUS

But what difference does it make? If people wish to use her old title, out of courtesy . . .

PHARNABAZUS

Your sister is the past, and should be discreet. We live in different times. Besides, Ephesus is much too provincial, too undistinguished a city to have an empress living here, particularly a *Greek* empress.

In the torches' glare, Herostratus and Pharnabazus face one another, Greek against Persian.

HEROSTRATUS'S VOICE

I had not realized until then that you were no longer honored among the Persians. But I was not surprised. How can one ever be surprised by what the Persians do? Their cruelty is notorious, and as they grow steadily weaker they will try to destroy us because they know that we are civilization while they are barbarians, elegant evil children of the long Asian night.

Then the two men are joined by Demetrius the High Priest. He is exquisitely tactful with the Persian Satrap, and rather offhand with the Greek poet.

DEMETRIUS

A splendid occasion, my dear Satrap, made all the more significant, if I may say so, by your presence here.

PHARNABAZUS

Simply my duty, High Priest. And of course . . . pleasure.

Pharnabazus looks at Herostratus, as though expecting a response. There is none.

DEMETRIUS

I have known her imperial majesty all her life . . .

Herostratus expects the "imperial majesty" to be challenged by Pharnabazus but the Satrap is all polite attention; he even lowers one huge ear toward Demetrius's thin mouth, in order to hear better that silver voice which has been carefully pitched, as usual, just below what might be easily heard.

DEMETRIUS

. . . and I find her now not only more beautiful than ever but somehow—what is the word? *Deeper*. One can see in her eyes something that was not present before, the spirit, in fact, of the goddess whose humble, unworthy servant I am.

HEROSTRATUS'S VOICE

The depths of Demetrius's hypocrisy can never be plumbed. He is High Priest the way other men are merchants. If he has any passion in life it is to move in great circles. He detests being Greek —and of the lowest class but one. I suspect he would secretly like to be a Persian noble and attend the Emperor day and night, on the ground that to be always at the side of the brother of the sun and moon ought to make one at least cousin to a star and so eternal.

47

NOW

As much as I dislike those who try to identify fictional characters, I find myself wondering who—and what—Eric has in mind. I assume he is somewhat identified with Herostratus, though I cannot think why if I recall the myth correctly. But his description of Demetrius makes me think of Fryer Andrews who just rang up to say that he was in Rome and would drop by. Fryer is a poet who neglects to write poetry and so should be honored for continence if nothing else. He was also one of Eric's teachers at Dartmouth.

The tone of Demetrius's speech is pure Fryer. He is a passionate social climber. But then, as Henry James once noted, the pursuit of a social career is as reasonable an aim as any other.

If Demetrius is aware of Herostratus's fierce thoughts, he betrays nothing. The beautiful voice whispers on.

DEMETRIUS

It is a marvelous mingling of the royal and the spiritual—look at those eyes! She is even more beautiful than her sister, the Queen of Caria.

Pharnabazus is again keeper of the tablets.

PHARNABAZUS

Six years ago, according to the treaty of Halicarnassus, Maussollus ceased to be King of Caria. He is now Satrap which means that his wife Artemisa is not Queen though she may use the courtesy title of princess by special decree of the Emperor.

Demetrius raises both hands as though to ward off a feather's blow.

DEMETRIUS

My dear Satrap, you must allow us Greeks our hyperbole! It is natural to us, a racial fault. Of course we know that all things flow from the Emperor, just as the sun itself, his brother, comes to us, as does he, from the east, to light our poor dark western land.

HEROSTRATUS'S VOICE

That I did not kill Demetrius last night will torment me forever! Pretending to be treacherous, we Greeks are simply servile in the presence of our masters, particularly Demetrius and his priests who have betrayed us a thousand times. But I take some pleasure in knowing that soon Persia will fall, and all the world will be Greek. We cannot be contained.

NOW

Suddenly curious, I have just taken a look at the *Encyclopaedia Britannica* to see if any of Eric's characters existed or not. Artemisa did. Helena did not. Herostratus did. Pharnabazus did not. Bagoas did. So far Eric's reconstruction is plausible. That is to say, the Persian Satrap might have been like Pharnabazus and certainly the Great King (who indeed had several dozen wives) could have been married to someone like Helena.

The script itself is something of a surprise. I had always thought of Eric as being essentially visual. Apparently not, at least so far. I keep thinking of Robert Wise's *Helen of Troy* in which Menelaus so memorably introduces the Trojan Paris to his court. "Paris, I want you to meet Achilles, Patroclus . . . Ajax, here, you know . . ."

The Bedroom of Helena.
In the small room, Helena lies on an ivory bed. Herostratus
sits beside her on a low stool.

HEROSTRATUS

Why should the Emperor want to kill you?

HELENA

Not me, the child. And not the Emperor really,
not Ochus. I think—I *know* that he is attracted
to me.

Helena's tears dry at the thought. She arranges her hair.

HEROSTRATUS

Then why are you so afraid? And who are you
afraid of?

HELENA

Bagoas, the eunuch. He is the most powerful man
in the world. Ochus listens only to him.

HEROSTRATUS

And he wants you dead?

HELENA

No, not me. The child. My son who should be
emperor.

Herostratus is alarmed.

HEROSTRATUS

Don't say things like that.

HELENA

But it's true. It was what my husband wanted.

HEROSTRATUS

I don't believe it.

HELENA

Are you for me, or against me?

HEROSTRATUS

I want you to survive.

Herostratus suddenly throws back the curtain at the door. There is no one in sight.

HEROSTRATUS

See? They don't even spy on you.

HELENA

Are you trying to say that I no longer matter? That the future emperor of Persia is nothing? That . . .

HEROSTRATUS

You matter to *me*. And, incidentally, Pharnabazus tells me you are not to call yourself empress . . .

HELENA

But that is my title.

HEROSTRATUS

He says not. Besides, you're Greek, and we have no emperors. To be Helena, daughter of Lagus is quite enough . . .

HELENA

What you are trying to tell me is that I must now give precedence to Artemisa. You would like that, wouldn't you? And so would she. Artemisa is Queen of Caria while Helena is simply a daughter of Lagus.

HEROSTRATUS

You are both daughters of Lagus. But you are greater than Artemisa—because you are Greek again while she is a Persian Satrap's wife.

This stimulates Helena's self-pity.

HELENA

Artemisa has always been luckier than I. Settling for so much less, she has gained so much more. I have lost everything. My husband whom I loved . . .

HEROSTRATUS

Helena . . .

But Helena is ravished by her own mythmaking.

HELENA

Loved, I tell you, with all my heart! And he preferred me to all his other wives.

HEROSTRATUS

Since he had fifty-eight wives, that is certainly a tribute. I'm told he could never remember their names. But then of course he was nearly seventy years old when you married him.

HELENA

He remembered my name. Besides there were only twenty women that could be called wives, even by Persian standards. Concubines is the correct word for *them*, but not for me. I was Empress.

HEROSTRATUS

At the end you were only a wife.

HELENA

How much do you know?

HEROSTRATUS

Artemisa has a very good ambassador at Susa.

HELENA

That filthy Greek spy!

HEROSTRATUS

You and I are both filthy Greeks. Stop pretending you are Persian.

HELENA

How can I *not* be Persian when my son . . .

Herostratus stops her, abruptly.

HEROSTRATUS

You used to take my advice . . .

Helena shifts ground. She becomes affectionate.

HELENA

Because you were my only friend. You took my
side against Artemisa. Against my mother. You
are the only person in this second-rate city that I
can bear to talk to, and the only one I missed
when I was at Susa.

*Herostratus has taken her hand during this. A moment of
tension. As if each is not quite certain what he feels.*

HEROSTRATUS

Then listen to me now. You are not to talk of the
child as being Mnemon's heir . . .

HELENA

But he is!

HEROSTRATUS

He is not, and you know it. Emperors do not
leave empires to three-year-olds . . .

HELENA

I was to be regent.

HEROSTRATUS

Then it is a wonder to me you have survived this
long.

HELENA

To me, too. Where can I go? I've thought of
Sicily but . . .

HEROSTRATUS

If you'd been regent, I can only tell you that

Ochus would have had you strangled within an hour of your husband's death.

HELENA

But I've told you. He is . . . fond of me.

HEROSTRATUS

He is more fond of being Brother of the Sun and Moon.

HELENA

Anyway I know him. You don't. He would never act openly. He would leave the job to Bagoas.

HEROSTRATUS

Has he?

HELENA

I think so.

HEROSTRATUS

To kill the child? Or you?

HELENA

Both.

HEROSTRATUS

Then go to Halicarnassus. That is the only place you'll be safe. Ochus fears Maussollus.

HELENA

Go to my sister? I prefer to die here . . . this minute . . .

HEROSTRATUS

Perhaps *you* would. But is it fair to the child? To let him die, too?

Helena is again in tears.

HELENA

Advise me. Help me.

HEROSTRATUS

I have advised you. Go to Halicarnassus.

HELENA

No.

HEROSTRATUS

Then renounce your title. Renounce all claim your child might have to the throne.

HELENA

If I did, would that satisfy Bagoas?

HEROSTRATUS

Why not? You have no money, no army, no allies. You are no threat to Ochus or to anyone except yourself.

HELENA

As long as I live, I am a threat. You don't seem to realize what a powerful legend I am in Persia.

HEROSTRATUS

You are a legend here, too. If that's what you want.

HELENA

I'm hated here. I always have been.

HEROSTRATUS

Nonsense. You, Artemisa and the temple of Diana are the three wonders of Ephesus.

HELENA

All the more reason for the people to hate us. Which is why I prefer the Persians, who worship me, to the Greeks who detest all distinction in others.

HEROSTRATUS

I know the mood. It will pass.

HELENA

I am another Helena of Troy to the Persians.

HEROSTRATUS

Helena without Paris. Or is there a man somewhere? Someone I don't know.

HELENA

There is no one. Anywhere. And as long as Persia's Greek Empress and her child Cyrus live, Ochus is not safe upon his throne.

HEROSTRATUS

Keep saying that and you *will* be strangled. With a silken cord, isn't it?

HELENA

Take me to Sicily.

HEROSTRATUS

You have no money.

HELENA

I have a little. And Lagus will give me more.

HEROSTRATUS

Our father sent out four ships in the last year. All four sank. It is a record, they say. Poseidon has never disliked anyone so much. That's why the house is full of seaweed and tridents, to propitiate the god. But of course it's too late. The ships are lost. Our father is poor. Why don't you marry again?

HELENA

I am dowager Empress of Persia, no matter what the local governor says, and I'm not about to give that up. Besides there is Cyrus. I want him to live to be . . .

HEROSTRATUS

Don't say it. Enough that he lives. Meanwhile, find him a suitable stepfather. In Sicily.

Helena is perverse.

HELENA

Sicily is so far from Persia.

HEROSTRATUS

It's no use. I can't help you.

Helena is reasonable.

HELENA

Don't. Don't get impatient. I know I'm not making sense. I've always been emotional. Not like Artemisa. I could never be cold like her, always calculating. Did you know *she* wrote the Treaty of Halicarnassus herself, without any help from anyone? My husband said she was worth ten satraps. But then she is masculine, and I'm not. If I had been I might have prevented . . .

Helena stops.

HEROSTRATUS

Prevented what?

HELENA

My husband's last marriage.

HEROSTRATUS

To Atossa?

HELENA

I was a mother—or at least a sister—to that girl. She was only twelve years old when I came to Susa. Her mother had been one of Mnemon's wives, briefly—an Armenian woman who always smiled. You know the kind. Anyway the day I moved into the palace, the woman came to me on her belly and asked me to be kind to her daughter Atossa. And I was. I practically adopted the girl, and oh, how the Emperor complained! "Why do you always have that squint-eyed child beside you when I come to visit?" Atossa is actually cross-eyed, a mark of great distinction in Armenia. But this was Susa, and it never oc-

curred to me that Atossa was anything but a
rather plain girl on whom I had taken pity. What
a fool I was! Artemisa would never have made
that mistake. "Great King," I used to say, "have
pity on the child. After all, she is your daughter.
You loved her mother once." Well, he took my
advice. Literally! On her fifteenth birthday he
married her and made her Empress and I was
forced to join the other wives in the south wing
of the new palace.

HEROSTRATUS

He must have been a monster, to marry his own
daughter.

Helena is indifferent to Greek moralizing.

HELENA

The Emperor can marry anyone. Look at the
Pharoahs. They marry their sisters.

Herostratus smiles.

HEROSTRATUS

Then marry me.

HELENA

Don't be absurd. All that I am saying is that to
be royal is to be different. We are like the gods
in our comings and goings.

HEROSTRATUS

You are Helena, daughter of Lagus, and no god.

HELENA

I *was* a goddess, and, oh, it is bitter to be a mortal
again, and afraid.

Helena's lady-in-waiting draws back the curtain. Beside her is Lysander, carrying a letter

HELENA

Come in, Lysander. Dear friend.

The lady-in-waiting withdraws

LYSANDER

Empress, I have a letter from the Queen of Caria . . .

HELENA

Does she know that I am here?

LYSANDER

What sort of an ambassador do you think I am? By tonight she will have received a full report.

HEROSTRATUS

I think Helena should go to Halicarnassus.

LYSANDER

Exactly what I have recommended.

HEROSTRATUS

But will Artemisa take her in?

LYSANDER

The Empress is her sister.

HEROSTRATUS

In our family that would be an excellent reason for *not* helping her.

HELENA

You are wicked. But it's true, Lysander. She's always envied me.

LYSANDER

She loves you more than anyone in the world, except King Maussollus.

HEROSTRATUS

You know our family, Lysander. Will Artemisa give Helena asylum?

.ysander is deliberate.

LYSANDER

I have every reason to believe that she would be delighted to have her sister live at Halicarnassus.

3ut Helena has her own interpretation of this generosity.

HELENA

In exile. Without money. Completely dependent on her. I would rather stay here with our mother.

HEROSTRATUS

You've only been here one day. By tomorrow you will have quarreled with Arsinoë, and be ready to move on. Anyway, I'll also write Artemisa, and ask her not to gloat too openly over your bad luck.

HELENA

And remind her I am still the mother of Cyrus who one day will be Emperor . . .

LYSANDER

Dear heaven, don't say that!

HELENA

But according to the oracle at Didyma, Apollo said very clearly that . . .

HEROSTRATUS

Forget the oracle and think about yourself, and Artemisa . . .

Lysander holds up the letter.

LYSANDER

. . . who is in good health and asks me to present a friend of hers to Lagus, the Egyptian Achoris.

HEROSTRATUS

The one who owns half of Egypt?

LYSANDER

Yes. And a good deal of Caria.

HELENA

I've never understood Artemisa's liking for merchants . . .

HEROSTRATUS

Stop being a goddess. All Greeks like merchants. What do you think our father is?

HELENA

At Susa no one whose family was not noble for three generations could speak to me.

63

LYSANDER

The court of Caria is only a pale reflection of that
of Susa . . .

HEROSTRATUS

What are we to do with Achoris?

LYSANDER

Simply receive him. He'll be in Ephesus for the
rest of the month. I don't think I betray any
secrets when I tell you that not only is he King
Maussollus's financial adviser but without his
loan the new capital could not have been built.

HEROSTRATUS

Then we must try to get some money out of him.

HELENA

We? What do you need money for? You live at
home. You do nothing except—what do you do?

LYSANDER

We all wonder that. Your brother is the most
mysterious man in Ephesus.

Herostratus is demure.

HEROSTRATUS

I spend a great deal of time at the temple, pray-
ing.

HELENA

I don't think that's at all in good taste. You
Greeks are so blasphemous.

64

HEROSTRATUS

I am writing a play.

HELENA

I heard the last one was not good.

HEROSTRATUS

This one is worse. It will be done at the spring festival. Electra and Orestes.

HELENA

You should really learn to read Persian. We have so many marvelous stories! There's one I particularly like . . .

HEROSTRATUS'S VOICE

You wondered what I did.

The City of Ephesus.
Herostratus moves through crowded streets and narrow lanes. At various points he meets men. One stands at the base of the water clock in the Agora. Another waits in an arcade. A third works metal in a shop. They exchange only a few words with Herostratus who moves on quickly, warily, as though he fears detection.

HEROSTRATUS'S VOICE

Now you know. Now everyone knows.

Theatre of Ephesus.
Actors are on stage, rehearsing a comedy by Menander. On the top tier of seats, Herostratus sits with two young men. They talk in low voices.

FIRST CONSPIRATOR

It is true.

SECOND CONSPIRATOR

I saw the order myself.

HEROSTRATUS

What did Pharnabazus say?

FIRST CONSPIRATOR

What could he say? He must obey the Emperor.

HEROSTRATUS

But when?

SECOND CONSPIRATOR

According to the order, all satraps must dismiss their mercenaries before the next rising of the moon.

HEROSTRATUS

Including Maussollus?

SECOND CONSPIRATOR

Particularly Maussollus.

HEROSTRATUS

In ten days time there will be a new moon. And on that day we shall drive the Persians out of Ephesus.

In silence the three regard one another.

The Baths of Poseidon.
Herostratus, nude, enters the circular steam room. Shadow-

figures move through s
to a large figure drawn
wall. Not until Herostra
features of Lysander becom

HEROST

In ten days.

LYSANDER

Good.

HEROSTRATUS

The money?

LYSANDER

It should arrive from Caria tomorrow.

HEROSTRATUS

Then meet me at the temple. At sundown.

LYSANDER

I shall be there. You've heard about the edict?

HEROSTRATUS

Yes. Without mercenaries, no satrap can govern. But what about Maussollus? Will he obey the Emperor?

LYSANDER

The King will obey. The Queen will not.

HEROSTRATUS

I hope Artemisa prevails.

67

LYSANDER

Between us, she is the real King of Caria.

HEROSTRATUS

If Caria went into rebellion at the same time we seize Ephesus . . .

LYSANDER

Persia would collapse. There is also good news from Rhodes and Athens. Their fleets will come to our aid *if* you depose Pharnabazus.

HEROSTRATUS

Tell the fleets to stand by. We cannot fail. Not now.

LYSANDER

And then you will be Lord of Ephesus. How proud Queen Artemisa will be!

HEROSTRATUS

What will Maussollus do when Ephesus is free?

LYSANDER

Join you in a league against Persia.

HEROSTRATUS

What assurance do I have of his aid?

LYSANDER

We have financed you for two years. What more assurance do you need?

Herostratus

You are a friend, Lysander.

Lysander

I am a friend to your whole family. To me the children of Lagus are the dream of the Hellenic spirit come to life and you, Herostratus, were born to lead the Greeks of Asia from slavery to freedom! So what can *I* do but follow? and record for history your great deeds.

NOW

I wonder how Eric could have *known* Lysander. His family were not political though Mr. Van Damm was briefly something of a power in the Republican party and was to have served in Willkie's cabinet had there been such a thing.

As I write the word "Willkie," I suddenly feel the summer heat of Philadelphia thirty years ago. I am at the Republican Convention with my grandfather (though a Democratic Senator, he attended all conventions with an excitement which proved contagious).

In a hotel suite I join a group of delegates come to meet Willkie. He stands in front of a window as people file past him, shaking hands. He is a white-faced, soft-looking, sweaty man (This was pre-air conditioning. Senator Vandenberg's supporters passed out fans which said "Fan with Van"; few did). Willkie is smaller than I'd expected. He never stops talking, like a wound-up toy. I can still hear his croaking tired voice say: "Ahd be a lahrr if ah said ah diddin wan be Prez Nigh Stays." The Hoosier accent is charming if somewhat calculated after all his years as a Wall Street lawyer.

Eric's father was also at the convention; doubtless lis-

tening with pleasure to the people in the galleries chant-
ing "We Want Willkie!" a somewhat cheap echo of a
radio comic's tag "We Want Cantor."

To my grandfather's disgust, I left the day before
the actual nomination, wanting to get back to Washington and my first affair—a better reason than usual for I
always tend to vanish at a certain point on public occasions. In 1960, as a New York delegate to the Democratic Convention, I seldom went near the Sports Arena
though I wanted Kennedy to win; yet when he did, I
felt like Murray Kempton whom I found, drooped
sadly over his typewriter. "Is this," he cried, "*all* there
is to it?"

Afterwards, Arthur Schlesinger, Jr., J. K. Galbraith
and I had a triumphant supper at a Polynesian restaurant in Beverly Hills, only slightly shadowed by the
bitterness of Stevenson's supporters, one of whom had
just accused Arthur of being the greatest traitor since
Benedict Arnold. In mid-feast I thought suddenly of
Eleanor Roosevelt's last appeal to the convention. We
were making a mistake, she had said, waving a long
finger at us, if we did not nominate Stevenson. But no
one had listened. Her passion for Stevenson was the
source of many cruel jokes and her loathing of the
Kennedys thought to be unfair: the father's sins ought
not to pass to the next generation.

With a twinge of guilt, and some malice, I asked my
companions, "*Have* we made a mistake?" Certainly
not! They were euphoric. As we left the restaurant,
Ken grabbed the ship's wheel which decorated the
entrance and spun it, shouting, "This is the ship of
state!" The spokes fell off.

I find it strange that Eric should have had any interest
in the sort of man who is attracted to the great. Yet the
type is probably more common than not, and to be

envied. Believing in a man, taking seriously a President, is to enjoy the security of childhood come a second time. But though man-worship is more reasonable than god-worship, I have never been able to light so much as a candle to another's glory—growing up in Washington was prophylactic.

The House of Lagus.
In the first courtyard, beneath a trellis of grapevines thick with green fruit, the family of Lagus is assembled. Lagus is methodically eating a dish of boiled sea gulls' eggs. Herostratus plays the flute, and watches Helena who is getting mildly drunk on wine, as her mother mounts an offensive in their old war.

ARSINOË

It is scandalous! There is no other word. The Satrap has been kinder than I would have imagined. But you deliberately taunt him. Just look at you! Dressed in those clothes, in those jewels, as if you were still in Susa, with your oily Persians.

Lagus has raised an egg to his mouth; puts it down; clears his voice to speak (to defend his daughter?); then thinks better of it; breaks open the egg, removes the yolk and pops it into his mouth. Helena needs no assistance. She is serenely magnificent.

HELENA

I am who I am, and cannot change for anyone. If you like I'll leave.

ARSINOË

It is obvious you cannot take criticism anymore. Lagus, speak to her. Explain to her what real life is all about.

Lagus is decently vague.

LAGUS

Real life?

HEROSTRATUS

Yes. Tell her what slavery is like. You forget,
Stepmother, that Helena finds it difficult to be a
Greek slave after having been a Persian empress.

ARSINOË

That's enough. You know I don't like that sort of
talk. It's dangerous. And it's not true. The Satrap
is a good friend to Lagus and me. We need him.
He does not need us. He has been most agreeable
about Helena, but he has his orders and I doubt
if he'll disobey them simply because this ridiculous daughter of mine cannot accept the fact that
she is but one of sixty widows to a barbarian emperor.

Helena takes this calmly.

HELENA

Dear Mother, you must never refer to the Brother
of the Sun and Moon as a barbarian. It is dangerous.

Lagus nods wisely; able at last to contribute to the conversation.

LAGUS

True.

ARSINOË

That's enough, Lagus. Go back to your sea gulls'
eggs. At the rate you eat them there won't be a
gull in the harbor by spring. Helena, what I say

is for your own good. You must also stop making
a spectacle of yourself in public. You were much
criticized yesterday when you went to the Persian
temple, dressed as a . . .

HELENA

I prayed for my husband, and for my stepson,
the Emperor Ochus. Who can criticize that?

ARSINOË

I can. Any Greek lady can. And does. You should
hear what they say! First of all you were dressed
outlandishly. Second the way you behaved with
the crowd . . .

HEROSTRATUS

Two thousand people came to watch her go into
the temple. You should be proud of your daughter.

ARSINOË

Proud of someone who displays herself like a
. . . like an *oriental* priestess? No, I am not
proud. My daughter is a Greek patrician, and she
should act like one.

HELENA

Like you, Mother?

Lagus sees fit to intervene.

LAGUS

Arsinoë is the very model of a patrician wife.

HELENA

That is because she is a shopkeeper's daughter,

73

and so must work very hard to appear to be what she was not born.

In a rage, Arsinoë is on her feet. She crosses swiftly to Helena and strikes her in the face. Helena responds by throwing the contents of the wine glass in her mother's face. Weeping, Arsinoë runs from the courtyard. Lagus remains seated, uncertain as to which—if either—side he ought to take. It should be plain that this is not the first scene of its kind.

HELENA

I hate her, Father.

LAGUS

Of course you don't.

HEROSTRATUS

After all, your mother found you your husband.

HELENA

Yes. She sold her daughters to the highest bidder so that she could be first lady of this stupid, provincial town.

Helena turns bitterly on her father.

HELENA

And you let her do it. You let her do anything she wants. And you always take her side against your own children.

LAGUS

That is quite unfair . . .

But it is now Helena's turn to go, weeping, from the courtyard, clutching her wine cup to her breast.

LAGUS

I hate scenes.

HEROSTRATUS

It is a sign of their love for one another.

LAGUS

Then I wish they would spare me these . . . demonstrations of love.

HEROSTRATUS

How can they when we are the audience for whom they act.

The two men are still for a moment. The only sound in the court is the soft crackling of eggs as Lagus rolls them between his palms to break the shells.

HEROSTRATUS

Why won't you help me, Father?

LAGUS

I have responsibilities. A wife. A family. People dependent upon me. If you fail . . .

HEROSTRATUS

We cannot fail.

LAGUS

I pray you don't. But I can do nothing.

HEROSTRATUS

Maussollus is helping us.

LAGUS

That is his concern. Not mine. And typical of
Artemisa. She loves making trouble.

HEROSTRATUS

A quality not inherited from her father.

Lagus sighs.

LAGUS

I don't understand these women.

HEROSTRATUS

I think you understand them better than anyone.
I think you created them. They are exactly what
excites you. Beautiful furies, tearing each other—
and now the world—to bits.

Lagus pursues his own familiar line.

LAGUS

A quiet life is all I ever wanted. I cannot bear
scenes. Politics. Glory. So what happens to me?
One daughter Empress, one daughter Queen. It
is a bad joke.

HEROSTRATUS

You have exactly what you want: a theatre all
your own, playing comedy, with you as privi-
leged audience.

For an instant Lagus reveals the face behind the vague
mask.

LAGUS

Then let us hope my imaginary theatre does not
suddenly change its policy—because of you—and
put on tragedy.

Herostratus's Voice

Comedy. Tragedy. We have known them all,
Helena. And more.

The Hill of Prion.
This low hill overlooks the gray-white city. On a plain
near the mouth of the Cayster River is the temple of Diana,
a vast complex of buildings, surrounded by a high wall.
Side by side on the turf lie Helena and Herostratus, making
love. Overhead the moon is full and white.

Herostratus's Voice

On the hill of Prion, we completed what we
began ten years ago when I told you that I would
love no other woman and meant what I said for
I have thought of no one else but you in all these
years, could not bear any touch but yours, for we
are as much the same as opposite: two halves
made whole by moonlight.

Lovemaking ended, they lie side by side upon the hill and
watch as clouds divide sky from dark earth and darker sea.

Helena

Now.

Herostratus

Now what?

Helena

I don't know.

Herostratus

I do.

77

HELENA

The two of us. And the child. We'll go to Sicily.

HEROSTRATUS

How would you like to be Queen of Ephesus?

HELENA

There is no such thing.

HEROSTRATUS

But if there were?

HELENA

I only want to be safe. So that Cyrus may grow up.

HEROSTRATUS

How would you like him to grow up here? With me as his father.

Helena is fond in her misunderstanding.

HELENA

As you were mine, when I was young.

HEROSTRATUS

I'm not that old.

HELENA

But you were that much older than I. You were . . . you are the only one I ever listened to. There was no one else.

HEROSTRATUS

Just as there is no one else now?

HELENA

Don't say that. It's not what I meant.

HEROSTRATUS

It is what you meant. And it's true.

Herostratus sits up. Distressed, Helena puts her arm around him. He shakes free of her.

HEROSTRATUS

I realize I'm simply your protector, and not a man at all.

HELENA

From the first moment that I knew my own mind I loved you most of all.

Herostratus is impressed by the gravity with which she says this.

HEROSTRATUS

Strange that I can never believe a word you say.

HELENA

Then believe what I *do*.

HEROSTRATUS

I am trying to. Particularly now that we have done what we were always meant to do.

Helena smiles; she is very beautiful.

79

HELENA

Like Egyptian royalty.

HEROSTRATUS

Can I trust you?

HELENA

Only with your life.

HEROSTRATUS

We are going to drive out the Persians. Soon.

Helena's alarm is not feigned.

HELENA

You dare not. You must not. You cannot.

HEROSTRATUS

Ochus has ordered all satraps to dismiss their mercenaries. The mercenaries are Greek. They will join us. In Ephesus we will outnumber the Persians ten to one. How can we fail?

HELENA

The Emperor's army outnumbers yours ten thousand to one. And he is merciless.

HEROSTRATUS

Other cities will join us. Rhodes, Athens—and Caria.

HELENA

Artemisa? *She* is involved?

HEROSTRATUS

We are financed by the Carian treasury.

Helena, as usual, has her own view of matters.

HELENA

So that's what she wants! To defeat me once and
for all. To put herself and Maussollus on the
throne of Persia. I should have known! There is
no stopping that woman's ambition, and hatred
of me. Ever since we were children she has envied
me. I was younger. I was more beautiful. I made
the greatest marriage of our time, and she was
always second-best. Now she hopes to be an
Amazon queen and seize what was *mine,* erase
my memory with her own. Oh, she is mad. I
tell you she is mad!

Herostratus has regarded this outburst with a certain
anxiety.

HEROSTRATUS

Artemisa has nothing to do with what we have in
mind. It is Maussollus who supports us through
Lysander.

HELENA

You know Artemisa as well as I do. She was
named for the Great Goddess and she thinks she
is the Great Goddess born again, and she won't
be happy until that temple down there has been
rededicated to her.

HEROSTRATUS

I think you are mad.

HELENA

I know my sister.

HEROSTRATUS

She is my sister, too.

This is all Helena needs to complete her vastation.

HELENA

Yes! And I am sure you would like to make love to her just the way you now make love to me.

Herostratus takes Helena by the shoulders and shakes her furiously, like a dog with a snake. She turns from tirade to tears.

HEROSTRATUS

If you don't conduct yourself sanely, we are all lost.

HELENA

We?

HEROSTRATUS

Yes. We. Because if anything should go wrong and I find you responsible, I shall say that *you* were my inspiration. That this rebellion was intended to put Cyrus on the throne at Susa, with you as regent.

Helena is truly shocked; as he intended her to be.

HELENA

You are a terrible man.

HEROSTRATUS

We are a terrible family.

HELENA

But I am innocent.

HEROSTRATUS

Continue to be innocent, and you will have nothing to fear.

HELENA

But I am afraid.

HEROSTRATUS

Don't be. As long as I live, I shall protect you. But you must protect me. You must say nothing to anyone.

HELENA

Who would I tell? I live in a house where I am despised, in a city where I am—

HEROSTRATUS

Adored. Wherever you go crowds gather.

HELENA

They are morbid. They enjoy the sight of a fallen empress.

HEROSTRATUS

You are a legend to them and simply to look at you makes them a part of the legend, too.

HELENA

You don't understand crowds.

HEROSTRATUS

I understand Greeks. And I understand you.

HELENA

When did Artemisa first get the idea?

Herostratus is sharp.

HEROSTRATUS

It was not hers. It is not hers. It will never be
hers. It is mine, as all the world will know when
Ephesus is free again.

Helena hardly listens.

HELENA

She has such power over men. I have never understood it. Look at the way she is able to keep
Maussollus under her thumb while openly having
an affair with that filthy Egyptian. What is his
name?

HEROSTRATUS

Achoris. And it is by no means certain that they
are having an affair.

HELENA

Lysander said they were, and he knows everything.

HEROSTRATUS

If she is having an affair—

HELENA

Why do you always defend her? I've noticed that
before. Nothing I do is ever right but if Artemisa
were to decide to make love to half the Carian
army you would say that it was necessary to im-
prove military morale.

HEROSTRATUS

I don't *always* defend her. And many things you
do are right. Such as what we did just now.

HELENA

My leg has fallen asleep. And my hair is a ruin.

HEROSTRATUS

If she is having an affair with Achoris, it is for
money. He is the richest man in the world.

HELENA

Caria is a rich country, too.

HEROSTRATUS

Not rich enough for what Artemisa has in mind.
She is building a new capital. Achoris loans her
money at no interest.

HELENA

Do you have any money?

HEROSTRATUS

When I am King of Ephesus—

HELENA

Yes of course. But I mean for now. Could we go

to Sicily together and have enough to live on, very modestly?

HEROSTRATUS

I have nothing. Do you?

HELENA

The jewels. A small allowance from Ochus. I am trapped.

HEROSTRATUS

Then let my arms be your cage.

Herostratus draws her close to him.

HEROSTRATUS'S VOICE

A pretty phrase, I thought, taken from the play I was working on. Unfortunately, what you wanted was not a fleshly cage, but one of gold.

NOW

Obvious question: Did Eric and his sister actually make love? Or is this simply a working out on the page of something that never happened? I suspect the latter.

The high romantic style of the scene is not altogether saved by the practicality of Herostratus, threatening blackmail. I should not have thought the Eric of the red notebook capable of writing a love scene so unexpectedly reminiscent of those ladies with three names who used to dominate the best-seller lists. Even in "historic" dramas, people don't talk like that while, in life, people almost never say what they feel. For most of us, it is the silences which express feeling, and perhaps inhibit it.

Recently I spent an afternoon full of silences in the Protestant Cemetery with someone I did not have an affair with a dozen years ago—too much silence at a crucial moment on a midnight beach, and a sense she was distracted by someone else—yet we continue to see one another year after year and affection grows, unstated and undefined and all the deeper perhaps for that.

Standing in front of the tomb of Goethe's son (whose billing is mysteriously larger than that of Keats on the various signs set out to guide us morbid pilgrims), I think how remarkably beautiful she is, as one marriage ends and another begins, and how we are once again together, in transit, emotionally. I prepare myself for the new husband, hopefully an improvement on the old, an emotional cripple who used her—much to her initial delight, it should be noted—as crutch, wheelchair, iron lung. But the masochism of women tends to be limited, and usually stops altogether when they give birth. Hers stopped, and so did the marriage.

Beneath ilex trees we stand for a time, observing an incredibly small hummingbird—dwarf among miniatures—hovering on fast wings an arm's length from us, plundering grave flowers.

We talk then of that recent biography of Lytton Strachey which revealed in such extraordinary detail the sexual and emotional lives of the Bloomsbury Group. She was most struck by Carrington (as an actress, she wants to play everything), the woman who lived with both Strachey and her lover in a happy ménage which only ended when Strachey died of cancer and she, not wanting to go on, took a shotgun and killed herself. "I shouldn't like doing that last scene," she confesses.

We ponder Bloomsbury, that bright short-lived world I have always found attractive. Particularly what our sociologists describe so elegantly as their "intrapersonal relationships." Certainly the complex private and public lives of those rare beings resemble not at all the way we live now, or—in America—ever lived. Of course my view of Bloomsbury is deliberately romantic, echoing Voltaire's similar dream: "What a delicious life it would be to share a home with three or four men of letters with talent and no jealousy, who would love one another, live agreeably, cultivate their art, talk about it, enlighten each other! I dream one day to live in such a little Paradise." So do we all, and never will.

Traditionally American writers have few lines of connection with one another. The country is too large, the philistinism too profound, the pseudo-democracy too fatally corrupting. It is no wonder that from the beginning the few good American writers were all, to say the least, a bit deranged as they tried desperately to conform life and art to the values of a peasant society which any European writer would have been startled to find a man of talent taking seriously.

Last spring I was much criticized when I said it is only because we are now a world empire that our writers are taken seriously. A number of reviewers brought up on *Moby Dick* (that masterpiece!) disagreed. Apparently American writing reflects our national genius, not to mention *the American experience* which so deeply moves our recent arrivals. Yet can anyone seriously compare Melville, Hawthorne, Twain —all we have of the near-first rank—with Pushkin, Tolstoi, Dostoyevski, Turgenev, Chekhov or with Stendhal, Balzac, Hugo, Flaubert or with Dickens, George Eliot, Conrad or, to turn to the modern movement, are Hemingway and Faulkner really working at the same level as Proust, Mann, Joyce? Even Ireland, a nation quite as provincial as our own and with a fraction of our population, has a literary history which puts ours to shame. Yet the American megalomania is now of such imperial proportions that reality no longer intrudes as we relentlessly display the clumsy products of our meagre civilization as paradigms for all the world to admire and imitate.

This unreality has had a bad effect on our writers who tend—like everyone else—to read less and less but when they do read are driven to the study of American writers. As a result *The Great Gatsby* is their idea of a masterpiece and the work of a Musil (or even Proust) unknown country not worth exploring. American writers want to be not good but great; and so are neither.

Perhaps the best aspect of Bloomsbury was the setting of standards not only literary but human and despite a wide range of vivid human frailties they made life and literature a good deal more meaningful than it ever was before in England, or ever will be in our perpetually—at least to those who must live there—foreign land.

They did their best work for one another, and who among us can say that he has any particular public or world in mind when he makes something? Or even any standards to uphold since it is the sense of this era that art should be play (echoing the least of Schiller's arguments), available to everyone, with no grades given because the idea of competitive skill is not democratic. "We all write books," said one very young writer recently, "but I guess we don't read much, you know, like they used to." Or care about much of anything, he might have added. But then we global villagers have no past, and cast no shadows.

"Will there be books like that about us?" she wonders.

"I doubt it. Not enough sources. For one thing we don't write letters. And they haven't started saving telephone conversations yet. But maybe the day will come. Can't you see a volume called *The Collected Telephone Conversations of Truman Capote?*"

"Except it will be a long playing record, not a book."

"Yes. No more books. A relief in a way."

We turn and walk through the green shade past marble angels weeping, intricate arrangements of metal flowers, a bronze plaque which records the death by falling from a horse in the sunshine of a young girl's days.

"We could be like"—she says it first—"Lytton and Carrington, what a wonderful life they had, except the end." We are in front of Trelawny's grave. I say nothing.

The House of Lagus.

The family of Lagus are gathered in the second courtyard with Achoris and his retinue. The Egyptian is tall and thin; his head is shaved. He could be any age that is not young. Although the eyes are large and splendid, the face is unpleasing, lips too full, nose bent to one side, long earlobes weighed down with Indian rubies. His voice, however, is remarkably pleasant.

ACHORIS

To Lagus, gifts from the Queen his daughter.

Achoris motions for an attendant to present Lagus with a chest which Lagus touches absently but does not open.

LAGUS

Very good of her, I must say. And of you to bring them.

ACHORIS

And to Lagus, gifts from a most humble Egyptian merchant, of no consequence at all.

Achoris motions for another chest to be brought to Lagus who this time gives it a small rap, as though to differentiate between the dutiful gift of a daughter and the gratuity of a stranger.

LAGUS

You are too kind, Achoris. You do us honor.

ACHORIS

To Helena, the dowager Empress of Persia, this small gift from an Egyptian no better than a slave.

Achoris holds out a gold collar fashioned to resemble a falcon. Helena takes it, her delight plain to all, including Herostratus.

HELENA

It is beautiful.

ACHORIS

It was designed for the wife of our late Pharoah. No one but an empress may wear it.

Helena puts on the collar.

ARSINOË

Actually our daughter may no longer use her title.

ACHORIS

I am sure my friend Bagoas will intercede with the Brother of the Sun and Moon to allow her to keep what is, in any case, forever hers.

Helena is doubly thrilled.

HELENA

You are as kind as we have been told.

LAGUS

Yes, indeed he is. Indeed you are.

Lagus claps his hands. Slaves appear with tables of food. Lagus is seen but heard no more as he settles in to dinner. Herostratus turns to Helena. They speak in low voices, as Achoris sets about charming Arsinoë.

HEROSTRATUS

Do you like him?

Helena touches the collar fondly.

HELENA

I like him.

HEROSTRATUS

A pity he is so hideous.

HELENA

A pity he is an Egyptian. Six of my husband's wives were Egyptians and they did nothing but make trouble in the south wing.

HEROSTRATUS

I can't believe that Artemisa sleeps with him!

HELENA

Why not? She would do anything for money.

HEROSTRATUS

Would you?

HELENA

I would do a very great deal for my son.

HEROSTRATUS

Would you marry me?

HELENA

If you take me to Sicily, right now, I will marry you.

HEROSTRATUS

Would you marry me if I were to stay here?

Helena is very hard.

HELENA

I would rather be what I am now, widow to an emperor, than widow to my own brother, killed by Persians.

The Temple of Diana.
Herostratus enters the temple enclosure. The main building is enormous, built to over-awe. Pilgrims from all over the Greek world file into the temple to look at the cult statue while the various altars before the temple are in constant use, their smoke smudging the blue day.
Herostratus enters the temple. At the far end of the nave towers the statue of the goddess, holding a child in her arms. The interior is splendid with different colored marbles and a ceiling of carved cedar. Herostratus crosses to Lysander who is waiting for him at the foot of the statue.

LYSANDER

The money has not come.

93

HEROSTRATUS

What's wrong?

LYSANDER

I don't know. It was promised for yesterday.

HEROSTRATUS

I am committed to the mercenaries.

LYSANDER

I know. I know.

HEROSTRATUS

They must be paid.

LYSANDER

What can I do?

HEROSTRATUS

What does Achoris know?

LYSANDER

Nothing.

HEROSTRATUS

What makes you so certain?

LYSANDER

Because Artemisa once told me that Achoris is very close to Bagoas, and could not be trusted.

HEROSTRATUS

Yet she was having an affair with Achoris.

94

LYSANDER

It is quite possible to have an affair with someone
you don't trust.

HEROSTRATUS

If only we could win him over.

LYSANDER

I wouldn't try.

At that moment Demetrius, dressed as high priest, sweeps
toward them.

DEMETRIUS

They said you were not coming but here you are
after all!

HEROSTRATUS

They?

DEMETRIUS

Your father and the Egyptian. Achoris is making
a gift to the goddess. He is most generous for an
Egyptian.

As Demetrius speaks, priests surround him; each takes a
ceremonial position.

DEMETRIUS

But then the daughters of Lagus are inspired by
the goddess herself and so work miracles. Achoris
is presenting us with a statue from Memphis. It
is plated in gold.

Demetrius gestures beautifully.

DEMETRIUS

Now we must go greet them.

Demetrius leads his procession of priests to the entrance.
Herostratus and Lysander follow.
At the first row of columns, they stop. From their point of
view, we see Achoris and Helena in the courtyard, surrounded by a large, excited crowd. It is quite apparent
that Helena is an even greater attraction than the gold
statue which glitters in the sun.
Demetrius approaches Achoris and Helena. Ritual greet-
ings, blessings, obeisances.

HEROSTRATUS

What does Achoris want that he does not have?

LYSANDER

To keep what he has, I should think. And he has
everything.

HEROSTRATUS

Why is he in Ephesus?

LYSANDER

Business. Why else?

But Herostratus is not listening. He stares at Helena who
in turn looks at Achoris with a bright steady gaze.

The House of Pharnabazus.
The Satrap is receiving Achoris, Helena, Lagus, Arsinoë.
Various Persian officials and Greek gentry are also present.
Dressed in the Persian manner, Helena has somehow man-
aged to maneuver herself into the only chair in the main
court which resembles a throne. But Pharnabazus seems

not to mind. In fact, he is unusually benign, delighted by Achoris.

PHARNABAZUS

At first it was quite a blow. How can any satrap hope to keep order without mercenaries? But then the Emperor authorized us to double our police force, and now I see the wisdom of his policy.

ACHORIS

He has insured a generation of peace for the Greek cities. It is now no longer possible for anyone to defy the Emperor, even though . . .

Achoris turns to Helena.

ACHORIS

. . . your people, Empress, have a positive gift for insurrection.

Pharnabazus allows the "empress" to pass. Helena rises pleasantly to the bait, with a set speech.

HELENA

I was born Greek but I belong to Persia, and my first duty is to my husband's memory and to his dream of a world at peace.

Lagus is not thrilled by this familiar pronouncement; but he is inspired to comment.

LAGUS

One thing about Ephesus: there's never been a rebellion in my time.

ARSINOË

That is because we have had wise satraps.

PHARNABAZUS

And the satraps have been fortunate to have such
loyal advisers as the family of Lagus.

With a bow, Pharnabazus crosses to the opposite end of
the court where a messenger is waiting.

HELENA

Of course Artemisa and Maussollus gave my
husband a great deal of trouble. It was particularly embarrassing to me when Artemisa started
calling herself Queen of Caria but . . .

Suddenly, out of character, Lagus speaks.

LAGUS

Family trait. Can't think why you two girls are
never happy to be what you are.

Helena gives her father a look of perfect hate. Achoris
moves into the breach.

ACHORIS

But surely they are happy to be what they are,
known from Ephesus to the source of the Nile as
the two living wonders of the earth.

ARSINOË

You shouldn't have said that, Achoris. She is already quite vain enough.

Helena is delighted.

HELENA

Do they really speak of us in Egypt?

ACHORIS

Why do you think I came to Halicarnassus? And
now to Ephesus? Only to see if what all the world
says is true is true.

HELENA

And is it?

ACHORIS

It is.

Arsinoë is irritated.

ARSINOË

Now she will want to know which is more beautiful. Artemisa or herself . . .

But Pharnabazus's return spares Achoris from making
judgment. Pharnabazus is cold, perturbed.

PHARNABAZUS

Rhodes and Phrygia are in rebellion against the
Emperor. Athens supports them.

NOW

A professional screenwriter would never begin a
scene with the announcement there will be no war, and
then end it with a declaration of war.

ACHORIS

We spoke too soon of peace.

PHARNABAZUS

Apparently. Now we must make certain that
Ephesus does not go the way of Rhodes.

ACHORIS

But if the Satrap is loyal to the Emperor there can
be no question of rebellion here.

PHARNABAZUS

With Greeks, there is always the possibility of
rebellion.

Helena's inadvertent display of alarm for Herostratus is
interpreted by the others as a normal response to sad
mutinous times.

ACHORIS

Fortunately, Bagoas will be in Ephesus tomorrow
to see me.

PHARNABAZUS

Yes. I know. A *secret* visit.

Achoris takes this with his usual bland amiability.

ACHORIS

I don't fear for Ephesus if you are so well-informed.

PHARNABAZUS

I am well-informed. And I fear for Ephesus.

Helena rises, very pale.

HELENA

I think, Satrap, we must go.

PHARNABAZUS

Be satisfied, all of you, that what I must do I will
do, no matter how hard.

On this equivocal note, Helena departs.

The Streets of Ephesus.
Persian soldiers patrol the streets. The citizens go about
their business, somewhat apprehensively for men are constantly being arrested . . . they are all Herostratus's fellow conspirators.

The Temple of Diana.
Dressed as a priest of Diana, Herostratus stands on the
porch of the temple, face hidden by a cloak.
From Herostratus's point of view, we see Helena arrive in
a litter; she is veiled and so does not attract the inevitable
crowd.
Descending from the litter, Helena motions her attendants
to stay where they are; then she crosses to the temple
porch. As she is about to enter, Herostratus stops her.

HEROSTRATUS

Do they know about me?

HELENA

Yes.

HEROSTRATUS

Who told them?

Helena speaks rapidly.

HELENA

They have arrested three hundred men. Any one
of the three hundred might have confessed.

HEROSTRATUS

I have been betrayed.

Helena ignores this.

HELENA

Achoris owns a ship in the harbor. It is called the
Ibis and it leaves on the first good wind for Crete.
Here is a letter to the ship's captain. And money.

Helena gives him a letter and a purse.

HEROSTRATUS

Pharnabazus could *not* have known about me.
Unless someone told him.

HELENA

What difference does it make?

HEROSTRATUS

To have been tricked by that stupid Persian
makes a great difference to me.

Helena starts to go inside.

HELENA

The high priest is waiting . . .

Herostratus takes her arm.

HEROSTRATUS

Will you join me in Crete?

HELENA

If I can, yes.

HEROSTRATUS

Is that a promise?

HELENA

That is a promise.

Helena goes inside the temple. Once she is out of sight, Persian soldiers appear. Swords drawn, they move toward Herostratus. He goes into the temple.

HEROSTRATUS'S VOICE

You had betrayed me, as I should have suspected, but did not.

Inside the temple, Herostratus dodges among the pilgrims; Persian soldiers block every exit. At the foot of the statue of Diana, Demetrius officiates, flanked by Helena and Lysander.

HEROSTRATUS'S VOICE

I had thought of you as wife, sister, other self, while you had thought of me as mere convenience, one of several possibilities and by no means the best.

Shouting furiously, Herostratus is now at the foot of the statue.

HEROSTRATUS

Whore! Whore! Whore!

But Demetrius, Helena and Lysander continue their ritual as if he did not exist. The pilgrims, however, are outraged by this impiety for it is difficult to tell whether it is the goddess or Helena that is being attacked. Then, as Herostratus moves toward Helena, the Persians seize him and he is dragged away.

HEROSTRATUS'S VOICE

If I had known then what I know now, I would

have killed you on the spot. But I did not suspect. How could I? How could anyone?

The Prison of Pharnabazus.
In chains, Herostratus lies on the floor of a stone cell. Lysander stands over him.

LYSANDER

What you must realize is that everything we have done was for your own good.

HEROSTRATUS

Was the money from Caria for your good or for mine?

LYSANDER

It was Queen Artemisa's idea. To help you.

HEROSTRATUS

No. Maussollus gave me money so that we might overthrow Pharnabazus and make Ephesus free.

LYSANDER

That, naturally, is the story we wanted *you* to believe.

HEROSTRATUS

That is the true story.

LYSANDER

The story which Pharnabazus believes is that Artemisa was simply financing her brother, to keep him out of mischief.

HEROSTRATUS

Phrygia revolted. So did Rhodes. Ephesus was about to. That is mischief enough for Persia.

LYSANDER

True. And the fact that things have gone slightly wrong in Phrygia and Rhodes is the reason why we were forced to bring a halt to your game—and an amusing game it was, too—I must say I enjoyed our conspiracy enormously: the secret meetings, the hopes raised, the hopes deferred, the . . .

HEROSTRATUS

You are lying! To save your skin you've invented all this.

Lysander is imperturbable.

LYSANDER

Pharnabazus will tell you that I gave him a full report of every meeting I had with you for the last year.

HEROSTRATUS

Then you are beneath contempt.

LYSANDER

I wish you wouldn't say that. I am devoted to your sisters . . . and to you, too, in a way. But you've always been difficult, you must admit that. You want glory like theirs not realizing that what they have is God-given and so beyond our envy or understanding.

HEROSTRATUS

I wanted only to make Ephesus free.

Lysander is suddenly sharp.

LYSANDER

With *you* as tyrant. And between Persian satrap and Greek tyrant I would prefer—as a Greek historian—the Persian satrap.

HEROSTRATUS

When am I to be executed?

LYSANDER

Your father spent the entire morning with Pharnabazus, guaranteeing your future good behavior—something I could not do, in all conscience.

HEROSTRATUS

I am better dead.

LYSANDER

I am sure you are, but you have powerful allies. The Empress and the Queen are formidable advocates.

HEROSTRATUS

I should have thought they would want me dead, too.

LYSANDER

Perhaps they do. But it would be a terrible blow to their prestige should you, a half brother, be executed by order of a Persian satrap. They have proposed exile. Anyway the whole matter will soon be decided by Bagoas once he has a free moment. He is a demon of energy that man! I suppose because eunuchs are thought to be slow and slothful, he is the exact opposite, and speaks perfect Greek.

HEROSTRATUS

What do you want?

LYSANDER

The Empress wants to know if you would accept permanent exile from Ephesus.

HEROSTRATUS

Did she suggest a place where I might go?

LYSANDER

As a matter of fact, she did. She mentioned— where was it?—Sicily. Yes. She specifically told me to tell you that it would please her if you went there, assuming of course the verdict is exile.

A long moment. Then Herostratus nods.

HEROSTRATUS

Tell her I am willing to go to Sicily.

HEROSTRATUS'S VOICE

That was the last time I believed in you.

The Council Chamber of Pharnabazus.
The eunuch Bagoas sits in the Satrap's chair. Pharnabazus stands beside him. Bald, large-nosed, Bagoas is thick-set

but not fat. In no way does his appearance or manner betray his condition. Achoris enters.

ACHORIS

Noble Bagoas, Vizier to the Brother of the Sun and Moon, accept my homage.

BAGOAS

In the name of the Great One whose slave I am, welcome.

The Satrap withdraws. Achoris and Bagoas stare at one another; then both burst into laughter.

BAGOAS

Well, you old thief, what are you doing here?

ACHORIS

Just reaping and sowing, as they say. And you?

BAGOAS

Intimidating the Greeks. How I hate them!

With some amusement the two old friends stare at one another.

BAGOAS

They say you're the richest man in the world.

ACHORIS

"They" exaggerate.

BAGOAS

There is only one way to find out. I shall arrest you, and hold you for ransom.

ACHORIS

If you did, there would be no wheat crop from
Egypt this year, and Persia would starve.

BAGOAS

You actually control the wheat crop?

ACHORIS

I control the market, yes. The weather, no.

Bagoas laughs.

BAGOAS

When we were boys I always thought that you
would be a king's minister while I would be
divinely rich.

ACHORIS

Shall we change?

BAGOAS

Too late now.

ACHORIS

And why should you want to? You have everything I have, as well as the power of life and
death.

BAGOAS

I meant too late because I have made a certain
. . . sacrifice, and there is no undoing it.

Briskly, Bagoas turns to a pile of correspondence on the
table at his side.

BAGOAS

The Emperor means to subdue Egypt once and for all.

ACHORIS

I know what he *means* to do. But will he?

Bagoas nods.

BAGOAS

What Mnemon lost Ochus will regain.

ACHORIS

And so you want my . . . what? Acquiescence?

BAGOAS

Support. We know the current Pharoah is your creation.

Achoris's voice drops an octave.

ACHORIS

He is the creation of Ra and Isis. Of the Nile itself. Of all that is holy—

BAGOAS

That is exactly the sort of thing *I* do extremely well. He is, however, your creature.

ACHORIS

So he is. Of course I will help you.

BAGOAS

Why?

ACHORIS

Without stability there is no world market. Without a world market there is no Achoris. Only Persia can achieve stability.

BAGOAS

I see no reason for you to lie to me—at least not about this.

Bagoas smiles suddenly.

BAGOAS

Now tell me, my old and treacherous friend, why are you in Ephesus?

ACHORIS

Business. What else? I have been touring the Greek cities.

Bagoas is amused at this evasion.

BAGOAS

I understood why you stayed so long in Halicarnassus . . .

ACHORIS

How the Greeks love to gossip.

BAGOAS

. . . with the lovely Artemisa.

ACHORIS

And how the Persians love to listen.

BAGOAS

I must listen to everything. Particularly anything which has to do with Caria. Maussollus could be dangerous.

ACHORIS

No longer. His health is bad and . . .

BAGOAS

But Artemisa's health is excellent, isn't it?

Achoris is bland.

ACHORIS

That is my impression.

BAGOAS

You old Egyptian ram! You've been making love to her right under her husband's nose.

ACHORIS

Under yours, too, it would seem.

BAGOAS

But then my nose is quite large enough to be everywhere.

Bagoas frowns.

BAGOAS

Your Artemisa is very beautiful. But not wise.

ACHORIS

I have tried to make her wise.

112

BAGOAS

She has been financing that brother of hers—

ACHORIS

Surely you don't take Herostratus seriously.

BAGOAS

Anyone who plots against Persia must be taken seriously.

ACHORIS

Even when all of us knew exactly what he was up to from the beginning?

BAGOAS

Because we indulged him for political reasons does not make his crime the less.

ACHORIS

What will you do with him?

BAGOAS

Kill him.

ACHORIS

I wish you would not.

BAGOAS

But I thought your affair with Artemisa was over. Maussollus said some very harsh things to you the day you left Halicarnassus.

ACHORIS

I knew it! The guard at the door was one of your
spies.

BAGOAS

No. It was the deaf-mute butler.

ACHORIS

Then you know that I am not allowed to go back
to Caria. So all the more reason for you to take
seriously what I have to say. Artemisa may be un-
wise but she is shrewd and willful. If you kill her
brother, she will retaliate, and you and I will
spend the rest of our lives trying to hold together
what is—at present—quite a good world for us.

Bagoas appears to be convinced.

BAGOAS

What shall I do with him?

ACHORIS

Let him go. No one will ever take him seriously
again, and that will kill him.

BAGOAS

Why are you in Ephesus?

ACHORIS

You don't like my answers?

BAGOAS

No. Even when we were boys, I could tell when
you were lying.

114

ACHORIS

And I've always known when you were telling the truth. It is such a rare occurrence that your face shines like the moon.

NOW

Bagoas is Murray Morris. I suppose Eric could not resist the caricature. Hardly a wise thing to do in a script meant for its victim's eye.

Bagoas is at first taken aback; then he roars with delight.

BAGOAS

You are the wickedest man in the world!

ACHORIS

No. Only the most practical—which of course seems like wickedness to the *im*practical. I have come to Ephesus to marry Helena, the daughter of Lagus.

Bagoas holds his breath a moment; then exhales noisily.

BAGOAS

Dangerous.

ACHORIS

For me? Or for her?

BAGOAS

Both. The Emperor detests her.

ACHORIS

Why?

BAGOAS

Why? You've listened to the woman! All that talk about the oracle at Didyma—how her son Cyrus will one day be emperor—how she was the favorite of Mnemon, which was not true by the way . . .

ACHORIS

She is very boring, I admit that . . .

BAGOAS

Then why marry her?

ACHORIS

For one thing, people don't realize that she is a fool . . .

BAGOAS

And you want to impress *people*?

ACHORIS

Don't you? After all, here I am a slave's son. An *Egyptian* slave's son. A self-made man, never accepted by the patricians—even though I have had as mistress the most beautiful of reigning queens. Now I would like, as a wife, the most famous woman in the world, the sister of my former mistress, the dowager Empress of Persia, who needs me even more than I need her.

BAGOAS

You are a surprising man, Achoris.

ACHORIS

You mean disappointing? Well, we all have our faults. Mine is wanting to possess things. I want people to look at me and say: the slave's son

116

sleeps with the widow of an emperor. He is now better than any patrician, he is part of history.

BAGOAS

I suppose if you don't listen to her, she is all right. Very well. You have my blessing. Somewhat mixed with pity!

ACHORIS

Thank you.

BAGOAS

This also solves the problem of Helena. Just last month the Emperor was talking about having her and Cyrus put to death, but I said no, it would distress Caria. When will you marry her?

ACHORIS

Just as soon as I've told her what I have in mind.

Bagoas is surprised, for the first time.

BAGOAS

You haven't told her you want to marry her?

ACHORIS

Certainly not. You don't think I would make such a move without your support.

Bagoas gives a loud cry, from the heart.

BAGOAS

And I gave it for *nothing!* You've tricked me again!

ACHORIS

Tomorrow I shall send you the deed to the island

of Thassos. It has a steadily improving annual
revenue, from marble, and a small but very com-
fortable summer villa.

BAGOAS

I am unworthy, but receptive.

Achoris is at the door.

BAGOAS

Achoris.

ACHORIS

Yes?

Bagoas is very hard.

BAGOAS

Never think of yourself as stepfather to a future
emperor.

Achoris is very bland.

ACHORIS

If you like, I shall dispose of Cyrus.

BAGOAS

I may ask you to.

ACHORIS

Easily done. I want Helena to think only of her
children by me.

In a good mood, Bagoas leads Achoris to the door.

BAGOAS

What would have happened had you become the
eunuch and I the businessman?

ACHORIS

You would be where I am, and I where you are.

BAGOAS

Yes. We would have each got the world one way
or another.

NOW

This is realistic if crudely put. People who obtain
power do so because it delights them for its own sake
and for no other reason. The American fantasy that
politicians represent, at best, Ideals or, at worst, Interests is nonsense but one is not loved for saying so. In
fact, whenever I discuss contemporary politicians I am
called cynical (my fourth century portraits, on the
other hand, are acceptable since that was a long time
ago). One despairs of ever communicating to people
what it is all about, the grim jockeying for position, the
ceaseless trading, the deliberate use of words not to
communicate thought but to screen intention. In short,
a splendidly exciting game for those who play it. That
little good comes of any of this—often as not much
human suffering—seems never to distress the believers
who choose to see in this politician or that true virtue,
and so take comfort in the cosmetic radiance of his
smile. No *good* men? No, nor bad either, at least not
often. Just men at play. With us as counters to be
moved about.

Of all the power-lovers I have known Eleanor Roosevelt was the most divided and so the most interesting.
On the one hand, she possessed the Puritan conscience:
she really believed that one ought to be good and help
others less fortunate. But she was also a spirited games-
man driven, like the rest, to prevail at any cost.

One hot summer night, there was a small dinner in

her cottage at Hyde Park, a few miles from where I used to live. Mrs. Roosevelt had just led to victory a Reform movement in New York City; she had brought down the leader of Tammany Hall, restored democracy. It was a high-minded campaign, and successful. Our little dinner was to celebrate the victory. Her son Franklin was particularly delighted by what had happened because the leader of Tammany Hall had, some years before, helped end his career in the Democratic party.

As we toasted our hostess, an angelic smile quite illuminated the beautiful luminous gray face with its swift shy glance (she would giggle nervously if you caught those small, clear, gray, pebbly eyes looking at you), and in her hesitant fluting voice, she answered our toast. "Years ago when Mr. De Sapio did what he did to my Franklin I vowed that I would bide my time and one day I would 'get' him. Well, I have!" So much for Reform.

Yet perhaps it is just as well that the people do not understand their masters and are drawn to support or attack them on frivolous grounds, much the way they like or dislike athletes and singers. For even if they knew what it was all about, they could change nothing. As it is, they are reasonably content. After all, slavery is the usual condition of our race as noted by—of all people—the emperor Tiberius. When the Roman Senate passed a law validating all his decrees thus far as well as any he might in the future make, he was horrified—what happens if an emperor goes mad?—but the Senate was insistent and so he accepted this *carte blanche* with the comment, "How eager they are to be slaves." Naturally, the ideal of the American republic was something else but it is not the first ideal to have been quietly abandoned.

To me the most astonishing phenomenon is not the power-man's desire to dominate but the human craving to believe—if not in Man—in a man. No doubt ape-watchers will tell us we are structured (this year's verb) that way. If so, it is a perennial tragedy since the world as prison is the ultimate conscious or unconscious dream of the man of power, with himself in complete charge, his voice alone reverberating over the loudspeakers. There is no substantial difference between Mao and Franco, Stalin and Hitler, Mussolini and Castro, Nasser and Salazar, only the rhetoric varies (and even that not much for nowadays each governs in the People's name) and though some power-men appear to be "nicer" than others, at heart they are as alike as rabid dogs, driven to infect the healthy, to assert totally their will. Nor is there finally any way of stopping them for they are truly the people's choice, the last assertion of our ancient tribalism which insists on homogeneity at any cost —all hair to be cut at an agreed-upon length while any violation of social, sexual, dietary tabus will be punished, because the good society is the *same* society, and variation is its enemy. With modern means of communication that ant hill commune which is the unstated (except by Mao) dream of every man of power can be achieved, and who would be so aberrant as to *not* want what the leader wants? After all, he would not be our master unless he truly embodied our secret longing for a totally ordered life without surprise or choice.

The House of Lagus.
Helena, Arsinoë and Lagus are in the second court. Arsinoë has a great deal to say about the proposed marriage.

ARSINOË

First, he is not Greek. Worse, he is Egyptian.

HELENA

My first husband was not Greek. And you approved.

LAGUS

Not quite the same thing. I mean look who he was.

ARSINOË

Achoris is the son of a slave. Don't deny it. I found out. Pharnabazus told me that his father had been a slave to the father of Bagoas. They were brought up together.

HELENA

Achoris is also very close to my stepson, the Brother of the Sun and Moon.

ARSINOË

Your "stepson," yes! What will the Emperor think of his father's wife marrying a slave's son?

Helena is euphoric.

HELENA

Bagoas approves. The whole world approves!

ARSINOË

Helena, is there *nothing* that you would not do to be noticed?

HELENA

Noticed! I want to hide from the world. I want to be invisible—and safe.

Arsinoë

So you marry the richest merchant in the world
who lives more grandly than the Emperor . . .

Helena

Achoris has promised me a quiet life, with everything I want.

Arsinoë

We know what that is! Adoring crowds and you
gracefully waving to them.

Arsinoë does a bitter and exact imitation of her daughter
greeting the multitude, the smile ruthlessly timid.

Helena

I am sorry that my life distresses you but it is
really no business of yours.

Lagus

Naturally you must do what you think right.

Achoris enters the court. He is more than ever eager to
please.

Achoris

Lagus, Arsinoë—I know what you must feel. And
I know that I have no right to want to include
myself in a family so glorious.

Lagus

Naturally you must do what you think right.

Lagus is serenely unaware of the repetition.

ACHORIS

But I am willing to relieve your pain, if that is possible. I shall be the best, the most indulgent of husbands.

Helena is purest honey.

HELENA

Even if you were not, in my eyes you would still be best.

ACHORIS

I have worshipped Helena from the first moment I saw her palely reflected in her sister's eyes . . .

ARSINOË

I am not sure that is the best possible beginning for a marriage.

Even Helena is somewhat dismayed by the reference; but Achoris knows what he is doing.

ACHORIS

No. I must tell the whole truth. I was delighted by the Queen of Caria, delighted to be in her presence, delighted when she turned to me for advice, and delighted when she proposed that I marry her sister.

Helena is startled.

HELENA

Artemisa proposed . . . ?

ARSINOË

It was *her* idea?

HELENA

I don't believe it.

Achoris extends a scroll.

ACHORIS

A letter just arrived from the Queen of Caria, expressing her pleasure that Helena has consented to marry me.

Helena is still uncomprehending.

HELENA

This was really Artemisa's idea?

ACHORIS

No. *My* idea, somewhat inspired by her.

HELENA

She is—incorrigible.

ACHORIS

Are you displeased?

HELENA

Oh, no. No. It is just that . . .

ARSINOË

My daughters tend to be critical of one another.

Achoris piles it on.

ACHORIS

Lagus, you will find in the harbor four of my ships that I have put at your service, to replace the ones lost to Poseidon.

LAGUS

That's very good of you, I am sure . . .

HELENA

Your prayers have been answered, Father! Poseidon has given back what he took away.

ARSINOË

Not Poseidon. An Egyptian "god" has given it back.

Herostratus enters the court. He has a week's beard and looks appropriately haggard from prison. Helena's somewhat melodramatic attempt to embrace him fails. He pushes her to one side. He turns to Achoris.

HEROSTRATUS

I said I did not believe it.

Helena deliberately misunderstands.

HELENA

But it's true. Achoris persuaded Bagoas to set you free.

HEROSTRATUS

Should I be grateful?

Lagus is suddenly practical.

LAGUS

Yes. Otherwise, you would have been executed.

HEROSTRATUS

It might have been preferable.

126

ARSINOË

You are as theatrical as your sisters.

In exasperation, Arsinoë turns to her husband.

ARSINOË

They get it from you, Lagus, not from me. There's proof. He's not my son.

HELENA

I think you should be grateful to Achoris. I am. We all are.

ACHORIS

I don't want gratitude but I would like your friendship, Herostratus.

HEROSTRATUS

I can give you my gratitude. But nothing more.

ACHORIS

I am sorry.

HELENA

Let me talk to my brother alone. Please.

The others withdraw.

HEROSTRATUS

You betrayed me at the temple.

HELENA

It was for your own good. Achoris said that

127

Bagoas would set you free. We thought it best to act quickly before you did anything desperate.

HEROSTRATUS

Did you tell Lysander that you wanted me to go to Sicily?

HELENA

Yes, I did. You would have been safe there . . .

HEROSTRATUS

That is not the reason you mentioned Sicily.

HELENA

I wanted you safe.

HEROSTRATUS

Safely away from Ephesus so that you could marry Achoris.

HELENA

I have no choice in the matter.

HEROSTRATUS

He can protect you, and I cannot?

HELENA

Yes.

Herostratus looks at her with wonder.

HEROSTRATUS

How can you let him touch you?

128

HELENA

How could Artemisa let him touch her? Though he swears to me they never had an affair.

HEROSTRATUS

At least that must please you: you've got him away from her.

Helena is unusually candid.

HELENA

As a matter of fact, what pleasure I might have had she has cleverly ruined. She is now claiming that it was *her* idea Achoris marry me.

Herostratus has not been listening; doggedly, he pursues his own line.

HEROSTRATUS

In Syracuse we could live quietly, you and I, and bring up the child . . .

Helena cannot resist the grand gesture.

HELENA

I would rather be with you in a hut than live in a palace with Achoris.

HEROSTRATUS

Don't exaggerate.

HELENA

No! I mean it. I take very seriously what happened on the hill of Prion. It was perfect. It was holy. And if I could do what I would like to do,

129

I'd leave with you this instant and go to the Pillars of Hercules if that was what you wanted.

HEROSTRATUS

You have been reading too many Milesian novels.

HELENA

Don't mock me! I mean what I say. You are everything to me. But I am the mother of Cyrus first and your sister second—

HEROSTRATUS

And Cyrus, if he is to fulfill the prophecy, must grow up rich.

HELENA

Can you blame me?

HEROSTRATUS

I can. I do.

HELENA

Then there is Achoris. He is the kindest man I have ever met.

HEROSTRATUS

Will you enjoy it when he makes love to you?

HELENA

I find him fascinating. Anyway that part is unimportant. He has admitted to me that since he has so many other women he is not apt to insist too often upon his conjugal rights.

HEROSTRATUS

You believed him?

HELENA

Dear brother, I lived at Susa, remember? With the Great King who spent days at a time in his harem, going from woman to woman and none of them me, but I didn't care as long as I knew I had his companionship.

HEROSTRATUS

You mean as long as you were Empress.

HELENA

I am no longer Greek like you. These things don't matter to me. Or to Achoris. He has also made it quite plain that I can see whomever I like, whenever I like.

HEROSTRATUS

Lovers?

HELENA

Yes.

HEROSTRATUS

Me?

HELENA

That is my dream, the three of us friends, together.

HEROSTRATUS

You are formidable.

131

HELENA

I must be to survive.

HEROSTRATUS

So it was all a dream. Sicily and us.

HELENA

There is a much larger dream now. You and I *and* Achoris! Think how splendid our lives could be!

HEROSTRATUS

When will you marry him?

HELENA

At the moon's last quarter. Naturally, Artemisa and Maussollus will be present. It is also possible that the Emperor himself will attend.

HEROSTRATUS

Will I be invited?

HELENA

I want you at my side.

HEROSTRATUS

But I am a known revolutionary.

HELENA

Oh, but no one takes that seriously. Not now.

Helena's tactlessness is more than Herostratus can bear.

HEROSTRATUS

Do you realize what you have done? You have made me a joke! The brother of the two sisters of Ephesus forever protected no matter what he does. Protected and impotent, kept on a leash like a pet lion—no, a sheep, a goat. I could kill you, Helena!

HELENA

Is this my reward? I saved your life and now you want to take . . . ours.

HEROSTRATUS

At least it would be something to have done.

Herostratus stops; aware of her use of pronoun.

HEROSTRATUS

What do you mean "ours"?

HELENA

I mean that I am pregnant. With your child.

Herostratus is too astonished to speak. Helena has at last carried the day; she condescends to be superb.

HELENA

That is why I must marry Achoris. That is why I want the three of us to be friends. For the child of Herostratus and Helena cannot help but be the wonder of the earth. So the oracle has told me, and so I believe. Now we have no choice but to love one another for all time.

HEROSTRATUS'S VOICE

For the sake of our child-to-be, I did not kill you.

133

I believed in the future you described. I wanted
to. And so I let go my pride, and was nothing.

House of Pharnabazus.
A reception is in progress. Helena and Achoris, Pharnabazus and Bagoas sit side by side on a dais. Dancers per-
form. The various courts of Pharnabazus's house are
crowded with Persians, Greeks, Egyptians.
Lagus, Arsinoë, Demetrius and Lysander mix with the
guests while Herostratus stands alone, very much Themis-
tocles at the feast. Helena and Achoris talk during the
dance, unheard by Pharnabazus and Bagoas who are busy
examining papers, demonstrating to the revellers that the
work of Persian officialdom is never done.

HELENA

You saw the Emperor's gift to me?

ACHORIS

No more than you deserve.

HELENA

Considering that the jewels belonged to me in the
first place, they are exactly what I deserve. When
I left Susa, Bagoas insisted I turn them back to
the Treasury.

ACHORIS

Now they are yours again.

HELENA

Ochus was always charming to me. You know, I
never felt I was ever in any danger from him.

Achoris betrays no amusement. His manner with her is indulgent and deferential.

HELENA

In fact, at one time, he actually discussed marrying me.

Achoris takes this invention in stride.

ACHORIS

To have been empress twice is nothing to having been, simply, Helena, the most beautiful of women.

HELENA

I would not have agreed with you—until now . . .

Helena turns upon him the full set splendor of her public smile.

HELENA

Now I am about to come into my own, as wife of Achoris.

ACHORIS

Where do you want to live?

HELENA

On the sea. Floating from island to island, belonging nowhere . . .

ACHORIS

Better yet. I shall build you an island and set it afloat.

HELENA

That will be even better than the city you built Artemisa.

Achoris

It will certainly be more expensive.

Lysander approaches them, distraught.

Lysander

King Maussollus is dead!

Achoris

How?

Lysander

The fever. It came on him suddenly. Two days ago. Just as he left Halicarnassus. But he insisted on traveling. Then, this morning, shortly before noon, he died within sight of the walls of Ephesus.

Bagoas has joined them.

Bagoas

Where is the widow?

Lysander

Outside the walls.

Bagoas

Who is heir to Caria?

Lysander

She is.

Bagoas

He designated no son? No male relative to succeed him?

LYSANDER

Everything is hers, Vizier.

BAGOAS

How large a retinue has she?

Bagoas exchanges a swift look with Achoris: two wolves contemplating a strike.

LYSANDER

The entire Carian cavalry and four cohorts of infantry.

Bagoas is disappointed by this foresight.

BAGOAS

They travel in state, these Carians.

LYSANDER

They had intended to make their formal entrance into the city tomorrow at dawn. But now—

HELENA

What will Artemisa do?

LYSANDER

She has not decided.

BAGOAS

We must try to persuade her to stay in Ephesus. Tell her we are most sensible of her grief, and so on, and we know that she will want to return immediately for the funeral but that since she *is*

137

here, I would be most honored to receive her. In
other words, a command but put it with Greek
tact.

During this they have been joined by Lagus and Arsinoë.

LAGUS

Most sad! Most upsetting! Particularly now.

Arsinoë is closer to hysteria than usual.

ARSINOË

I must go to my child! Lysander, take me to her.
Immediately!

LYSANDER

She asked, particularly, that no member of her
family see her tonight.

ARSINOË

But I am her mother!

HELENA

And that is why she would rather not see you
just now. I know exactly how she feels.

ARSINOË

That was unkind.

HELENA

But true. Lysander, did she ask for me?

Lysander is uncomfortable; but he soldiers on.

LYSANDER

Yes. She said she was sorry that your wedding
would have to be postponed.

138

HELENA

Postponed?

ARSINOË

Obviously. We must observe thirty days mourning.

HELENA

Achoris?

ACHORIS

It is the custom. And I think it wise. We want
the best possible auguries for the future.

Helena is shattered.

HELENA

Yes. Of course.

LYSANDER

The Queen also said that tomorrow she would
like you to come to her.

ARSINOË

Not me?

LYSANDER

I'm sorry. The Queen asked only for Helena.

Helena brightens; forgetting for a moment her disappoint-
ment at the wedding's postponement. She is one up on
Arsinoë.

HELENA

Tell her I shall come to her, gladly.

139

BAGOAS

And tell her I would like her to come to me. Sadly but politically.

LYSANDER

I am sure she will see the wisdom of such a meeting.

Achoris turns to Pharnabazus.

ACHORIS

My dear Satrap, I am afraid we must begin our mourning now. The entertainment is over.

The Camp of Artemisa near Ephesus.
A small army is encamped to one side of the main road. Tents have been pitched. Lysander escorts Helena to the entrance of Artemisa's pavillion.

The Pavillion of Artemisa.
On a bier lies the body of Maussollus. Beside it kneels Artemisa, hair falling loose down her back. For a moment Lysander and Helena simply stand and stare, awed by this tableau of royal grief. Then Artemisa rises, turns to Helena. She is more serious in manner than her sister, but quite as beautiful. She also possesses a mind, something the gods neglected to include among Helena's natal gifts.

ARTEMISA

The King loved you both.

Helena bursts into tears, as Artemisa intended. With a sob, Lysander tries to tear a part of his tunic to show grief but the fabric holds firm.

LYSANDER

The light has gone out of the Greek world.

ARTEMISA

We must remember him.

Artemisa takes Helena in her arms.

ARTEMISA

I had so hoped to see you happy, on your wedding day.

HELENA

Nothing matters now.

But mention of the postponed wedding brings Helena's weeping to an end. Artemisa motions for them to sit at the foot of the bier on which lies Maussollus, a handsome bearded man turning blue.

ARTEMISA

Is it true that Bagoas is in Ephesus?

LYSANDER

Yes, glorious Queen, sombre in your grief, as Demeter herself . . .

Helena is staring at Maussollus.

HELENA

To think we shall never again hear those lips speak . . .

Artemisa's response is somewhat perfunctory; she has other things on her mind.

ARTEMISA

As Homer says, he is happy. Why is Bagoas in Ephesus?

141

HELENA

He came for my wedding. After all, he is one of Achoris's oldest friends.

Artemisa smiles, a small sad smile.

ARTEMISA

You know it was my dearest wish that you marry Achoris . . .

HELENA

Our wedding will be all the sweeter, knowing it was your wish.

ARTEMISA

In fact, more than wish—conspiracy! isn't that true, Lysander?

LYSANDER

Yes. I was instructed to do everything I could to bring Achoris into "our" family.

HELENA

At first I was reluctant. The difference between us was so great . . .

ARTEMISA

But he is young for his age.

HELENA

I was not speaking of age but station in life . . .

ARTEMISA

Of course. Those years at Susa . . .

HELENA

Those beautiful bright years when all the world was mine . . .

LYSANDER

Nothing can ever take their place . . .

Artemisa's sense of humor is somewhat mordant.

ARTEMISA

According to our ambassador, the Empress Atossa was poisoned by Bagoas.

HELENA

Served her right, the cross-eyed Armenian bitch.

ARTEMISA

I must say you were marvelously brave to have endured those years at Susa, your life always in danger . . .

HELENA

My life was never in danger while my husband lived. But now that we are both widows. . . . Poor Artemisa, what will you do?

Artemisa is unmoved; her position does not strike her as at all poignant.

ARTEMISA

I shall govern Caria. It was my husband's wish. And I shall build him a tomb such as the world has never seen. It will make the pyramids at Thebes look like toys in the sand.

HELENA

Sounds awfully expensive . . .

ARTEMISA

What is money compared to the grief of Artemisa, widow of Maussollus? I have already given orders for the leading architects and sculptors of Ephesus to meet me tomorrow in the city.

LYSANDER

Then you will come into the city?

ARTEMISA

Why not? It is the city of our family. Unless of course you think there is some danger . . .

HELENA

Only from our mother. She has never been more hateful.

Artemisa turns to Lysander.

ARTEMISA

Is there danger?

LYSANDER

Not as long as your troops are just outside the gates.

HELENA

How can you be so practical with . . .

Helena indicates the bier.

HELENA

. . . with your husband dead? Your whole life changed.

ARTEMISA

Only by being practical can I keep my life from changing more than I might like.

LYSANDER

The Queen is wise.

HELENA

Poor Maussollus, cold, unmourned . . .

Artemisa rises to this challenge.

ARTEMISA

Unmourned! The world will never forget the grief of Artemisa.

HELENA

No doubt. But will they remember her husband?

The two sisters face one another across the dead man's body. Neither speaks for a moment, hostility and love so evenly balanced that neither is quite certain what she feels about the other. It is Artemisa who breaks the silence.

ARTEMISA

What is to be done with Herostratus?

HELENA

I've tried to talk him into going abroad. To Sicily.

145

ARTEMISA

He nearly ruined us all.

LYSANDER

I think Bagoas believed our story.

ARTEMISA

While my husband was alive he had no choice.
But now . . .

Artemisa does not continue.

HELENA

It was not wise of you to help Herostratus. You
know what a fool he is.

ARTEMISA

He almost made a successful revolution. He almost freed the Greek cities. I don't call that the
work of a fool.

HELENA

"Almost" to do something is to be a fool. But we
saved him. Or Achoris did, for our sake.

ARTEMISA

Achoris is a good friend.

HELENA

So I tell our brother who will not believe me.

ARTEMISA

Because he is jealous.

Helena is startled: what does Artemisa know?

HELENA

Jealous . . . ?

ARTEMISA

Of you. Of me. Of Achoris for being rich.

Helena is relieved.

HELENA

Yes. He is very ambitious. He wants all the world
to know his name the way they know ours.

LYSANDER

One can hardly blame him.

ARTEMISA

I had hoped he would succeed.

LYSANDER

We played a double game. If he won, the Greek
cities would be free, with our aid. If he lost, we
were simply keeping an eye on him, promising
him money he never actually received.

Artemisa has been staring thoughtfully at Helena during
this. When she speaks, she is delicate.

ARTEMISA

Helena, no matter what happens, I want you to
know that . . .

HELENA

Whatever happens?

147

ARTEMISA

. . . that for you alone in the world do I have
perfect affection—and understanding.

HELENA

We are trapped together, aren't we? You and I
forever, the two sisters of Ephesus . . .

ARTEMISA

And I will do whatever I can for you, and only
ask that you understand me when I do what I
must do.

HELENA

And what is that?

ARTEMISA

Save myself. Save Caria. Save the culture of our
people.

HELENA

You should have been a man. I've always said
so.

ARTEMISA

I'm sure you have. Only for what I must now do,
being a woman . . .

LYSANDER

A beautiful woman . . .

ARTEMISA

. . . is not a disadvantage.

The House of Lagus.
Artemisa is holding court in the atrium. She is surrounded
by architects and sculptors. Some have brought models of
the tomb for Maussollus.
Lagus and Arsinoë are crowded into a corner of the second
court, neither very happy. On the other hand, Herostratus
is amused.

HEROSTRATUS'S VOICE

You must admit that Artemisa is our family's one
true general. Within a day of her arrival at
Ephesus, she had won over Bagoas, charmed you,
flattered me, set in motion her plans for building
the most beautiful tomb in history—there is a
nice irony in the fact that she and I shall each
be immortal for a building—and, finally, she did
just what she told you she would do in the pavillion outside the walls. She saved herself.

During this, Achoris enters the court, makes obeisance to
Artemisa who motions for the artisans to withdraw. Lagus,
Arsinoë and Herostratus now join Artemisa and Achoris.

ARSINOË

I have never seen so many common people in my
life.

ARTEMISA

You have just seen the best architects and sculptors in the world.

LAGUS

Very nice in their place but not in the house.

ARTEMISA

I enjoy them.

149

LAGUS

Better than poets, I suppose.

HEROSTRATUS

Or revolutionaries.

The others choose to disregard this expression of bad taste. Achoris addresses Artemisa.

ACHORIS

I have come from Bagoas.

ARTEMISA

He was sympathetic?

ACHORIS

Delighted. Of course I gave him another island.

ARTEMISA

You have so many to give.

ARSINOË

What are you two plotting?

ARTEMISA

Survival.

Helena enters the court. She is even more resplendent than usual, very much the dowager Empress of Persia.

HELENA

I've just come from the temple of Diana. Deme-

trius tells me there is to be a ceremony of thanks-
giving tomorrow.

ARTEMISA

Yes. I've ordered it.

ARSINOË

With your husband dead only a week, you are
giving thanks? For what, may I ask?

ARTEMISA

Helena, you remember what I told you? that I
shall always care for you . . .

HELENA

Yes . . .

ARTEMISA

Remember it now. Be strong. Be worthy of our
legend. I am marrying Achoris tomorrow.

Arsinoë gasps. Lagus looks hungry. Helena is purest alabaster. Herostratus alone seems not to be surprised.
Achoris gestures apologetically to Helena. Artemisa alone
is composed.

ARTEMISA

It is no secret that he and I have long been
friends. But forced to choose between my husband whom I worshipped and Achoris whom I
loved, I chose my husband and sent Achoris here,
hoping he would marry Helena and so continue
to be . . . one of us. But Maussollus died. I am
alone in Caria. I need a man whom I can trust to

151

help me govern, to help me preserve the integrity
of our Greek culture . . .

At this moment, just as Artemisa slips unconsciously into
her politician's role, Helena walks from the courtyard, all
eyes upon her. Even Artemisa, professional spokesman for
Hellenism, is still. It is Arsinoë who finally speaks. She
turns to Artemisa with a certain wonder.

ARSINOË

I had never realized until this moment that I had
given birth to such a monster.

Artemisa takes the insult coolly.

ARTEMISA

If that were the only thing you had never realized, you would be wiser than you are now. But
let me instruct you further since you are in a
learning mood. You are nothing, Mother, while
we are everything. For it is us that the world has
dreamed, not you. And that I am monstrous in
your eyes is sad but of no importance, for the
Queen of Caria means to live out her legend and
be remembered for all time, and if she is, who
cares what womb she fell from, and in whose
house?

The Temple of Diana.
In front of the temple a great crowd has formed.
Trussed-up geese lie near the altars, ready for Demetrius
and his priests to offer up to the goddess. Bagoas and a
large delegation of Persians benignly watch as the colorful
Greeks indulge themselves in their arcane rites.
Crowned and bejewelled, Artemisa stands before the main
altar. Just behind her Achoris, Lysander, Lagus, Arsinoë
and Herostratus.

HEROSTRATUS'S VOICE

I did not know, as the ceremony began, how it would end.

Helena's Room.
Helena is with the child Cyrus and a nurse. She addresses the child solemnly but we hear nothing of what she says.

HEROSTRATUS'S VOICE

Because I did not know what you were about to do.

Weeping, the nurse and the child go.
In one hand, Helena now holds a mirror; in the other a knife. For a long moment she stares into the mirror, taking fond leave of that beauty which has given her and the world such pleasure.
Then mirror still in hand, she drives the knife into her heart and with a startled scream falls forward onto the floor, the mirror's face splashed with tiny drops of blood.

The Temple of Diana.
The ceremony is still in progress. The distraught nurse is trying to make her way past the guards to the family of Lagus at the foot of the main altar. Demetrius is addressing the goddess.

DEMETRIUS

Constant yet ever changing, the phases of the moon reflect your spirit, waxing and waning . . .

Herostratus sees the nurse. He motions to the guards to let her approach. As she tells him of Helena's death, Demetrius's voice continues.

DEMETRIUS

Mother of all men, yet pure and virginal. Mistress of the night, yet wife to the day, whose house is

153

here at Ephesus, the greatest and most splendid temple in the world, sacred to you for centuries, and for all time to come.

Herostratus's face shows first disbelief, then astonishment and, finally, rage.

HEROSTRATUS'S VOICE

You did not think of me or of our child-to-be or of the child whose future so much concerned you. You thought only of yourself and Artemisa. Of her victory and your defeat. There was nothing left for you to do but with a knife's blow gain the world's pity while shadowing forever the life of Artemisa. Oh, I know you so well! Your vanity is just like hers, like mine. To transcend death, you were willing to die.

Herostratus suddenly darts from the group before the altar.

HEROSTRATUS'S VOICE

Well, I can do better. I have done better. Watch me, eternity! Watch *me* become immortal!

Herostratus seizes one of the torches beside the main altar. Demetrius stops his invocation. All stare at Herostratus as he races up the steps of the temple.

Inside the Temple of Diana.
At the base of the cult statue, tripods support bowls of burning incense. Rapidly, Herostratus fires a series of hangings against one wall; then, as the first alarmed priests appear in the doorway, he upsets the tripods. Burning incense scatters in all directions. Flames climb the walls. Old wood crackles. With a roar, the carved roof beams turn to flame.
At the foot of the statue, Herostratus stands, waving his torch like a banner and shouting exultantly.

HEROSTRATUS

I have burned the temple of Diana!

Outside the Temple of Diana.
Smoke fills the door. The cry of "fire" begins. Priests and soldiers hurry to the temple. Horrified, Demetrius prostrates himself before the altar. The Persians are outraged by the disorderliness; the Greeks are stunned by the sacrilege. Only Artemisa is calm. With an air of wonder, she turns to Achoris.

ARTEMISA

Do you realize what Herostratus has done?

ACHORIS

Yes. He has set fire to the world's most famous temple, and no one can save him now.

ARTEMISA

Save him? He has saved himself. That fire will be remembered when Helena and I are nothing but faded inscriptions on broken walls. He has destroyed us, and got his wish for of us all, only he will be remembered now.

Like a widow who has just seen her husband turned to ash, Artemisa moves away from Achoris and her family.

The Prison Cell.
Herostratus is chained to the wall.

HEROSTRATUS

Poor Helena, what is an empress to a god? As I await the executioner, I know that I am being watched by future generations and I know that to the end of time they will discuss with awe what I have done and wonder why I did it, not knowing *that* is precisely why, why we do anything.

Herostratus now speaks not to Helena but to those who will come after.

HEROSTRATUS

So remember me, that I do not die. Forget the two sisters of Ephesus for what are they but simply witnesses to Herostratus? who burned the temple of Diana which was the wonder of the earth.

NOW

What did Marietta mean when she asked me if I believed in possession? I am afraid I know. It is very like her to want to believe that the spirit of Herostratus possessed Eric in order to appear as a character in a film to be produced by Murray Morris in 1948. Certainly the unspeakable Herostratus would be quite capable of wanting to be heard from again but Eric strikes me as a most unlikely medium. Admittedly he must have had something of Herostratus in him or he could not have written the character the way he did. But then the artist's desire to outwit death through perpetual fame is a common one, and no less powerful a drive for its naiveté. We all possess it to some degree, even Eric whom I plainly never knew.

Marietta lives in a world of supernatural powers. She has always been fascinated by spiritualism. She once spent a week in a copper cage guessing which cards were being dealt in a cottage some miles away. The results were inconclusive. Nevertheless, Marietta refers to herself as a "sensitive" and likes to quote the formidable Eileen Garrett who once told her, "Your true gifts are psychic not literary." Lacking irony, Marietta has never realized that Eileen's message to her occurs at the end not at the beginning of the sentence.

But any game can give comfort and a belief in ghosts is no sillier than a belief in art (as I write this line I mentally cancel it: art does exist, ghosts don't but I preserve the line since I can neither prove nor disprove the existence of either). Certainly in an age where the traditional religions are disintegrating (not fast enough for me) all sorts of makeshifts like astrology, scientology, drugs will fill the void. After all, there is nothing so absurd that someone will not believe it, which brings one to the question: are we made that way? Do our brains require the supernatural, the symmetrical god?

I hope not. I am not made that way—as far as I can tell. I accept, glumly, the fact of death as extinction in time and so take all the more pleasure in the living moment. There is no god anywhere in my mind, and no need for one. Yet I understand Marietta's belief in ghosts: if they exist then she, too, will exist after death, able to regard with perfect love her shadowy self for all eternity. This thought comforts her, horrifies me.

I have always known that not only are there plenty more where we come from but that the sense of uniqueness each of us has is the one thing which makes us most alike. We are interchangeable, born to reproduce and die, nothing more. At least that is what I would tell Marietta if she were here with me on the terrace; anything to disturb her self-absorption.

Of course there are other things the living do. We play games. That is our occasional glory. What game was Eric playing with Herostratus? With Marietta? With me? I study the screenplay for clues.

Only writers know how they use the "real" in their fictions and no writer has yet been willing or able to explain how he does it. Fortunately his testimony is no longer sought. We live in an age of explicators for whom the novel is not an act of creation but a mere reflection of the author's actual life which, with perverse (even neurotic) ingenuity, he has disguised, never realizing that he is certain to be found out for now there is no Xanadu so remote that some devoted Interpol academic will not make the journey, reporting to us on the state of the road, the people encountered, the books the author was reading when he first looked upon that stately pleasure dome, pleasure no longer for what was Xanadu, finally, but a troubled dream brought on by several grains of laudanum and the random reading of a disorderly life?

It is a pity that what pleasure literature might still give to the not so happy few who like to read is undone by the explicators. Even the most devoted young reader is not apt ever to want to look at another novel after "studying" the subject at any American university. And what madness to "teach" the works of contemporary writers who write not to be taught but to be read. It is like teaching conversation—not a bad idea come to think of it—or how to watch a movie.

Yet to a greater or lesser degree all writers reveal themselves in their works and if one is more interested in the writer than in what he has written, as I am more interested in Eric than in his screenplay, then the work is fair game for a literary detective.

Right off, there is the matter of Helena and Herostratus. Are they drawn from life? Were Eric and Erika lovers? If they were, then I must revise my own past.

THEN

I thought the script was just fine. I knew there was too much Herostratus for Murray but the girls were still the stars with everything to do from Madame Butterfly to Medea. How could he not like it?

I sent him the script the second I got it back from the typist (somewhat changed from the version you've just read in this notebook), and I waited for two days to hear from him. But there was only *omnious* (as M.M. would say) silence from the Prince de Galles.

On the third day I presented myself at the hotel and asked if he was in and when they said yes I went straight to his room and knocked on the door. There was no answer. I tried the door; it was not locked. I opened it and there, hanging by the neck from the bathroom door, feet off the ground, face blue, was Murray Morris.

"For God's sake, the script's not that bad!" Somehow it is not possible to take Murray seriously, even when he appears to have killed himself.

"Push . . . the . . . stool." I noticed a footstool just out of reach of his desperately pointing toe. I placed it beneath him. He then undid the complicated series of knots about his neck and stepped down. "I tried," he said, still gasping for air, "to ring you but you were always out."

Even at the point of death, Murray will lie. "I've been home for two days waiting to hear from you."

"They said you were out. It is not very responsible of you, going off like that without leaving word where you may be found. It shows a lack of *esprit de corps*."

I counterattacked. "Why did you hang yourself?"

"I did not hang myself."

"Murray, I *saw* you hanging from the bathroom door. If it weren't for me you'd be dead."

"I did not hang myself. I was *stretching* the arthritis in the neck. It is a new technique. And you did *not* save my life because all I had to do was step onto the footstool and get down."

"The footstool was out of reach. You were purple in the face . . ."

Suddenly Murray screamed his elephant scream; for an instant his nose even resembled a furled elephant's trunk.

"You're destroying me!" Then Murray grabbed the script and began to choke its neck. Yes, I know scripts don't have necks but if they did this is exactly what he was doing to "The Two Sisters of Ephesus."

"Filth!" He shrieked, letting the lifeless script fall to the floor. Then he sank into a chair and covered the top of his head with both hands, to ward off Jehovah's wrath or maybe mine for I was beginning to respond in kind, as they say.

"What . . . filth?" I asked.

Murray took a deep breath, steadied himself; the elephant's plangent tenor dropped an octave to Murray's usual con-man baritone, Vienna-style. "Baby, I am not a prude. I think you know that. Further, I am always attempting to push the boundaries of the cinema as far as possible toward reality, to achieve in a popular medium what literary artists like James Joyce and Franz Werfel have accomplished in their classic books, written admittedly for a very small audience but no less valid. It was a Murray Morris film that first used the word *urning* on the screen. It was a Murray Morris film that first used not one but two *damn*'s and I was not working with a classic property like *Gone With the Wind*. It was a Murray Morris film

that showed for the first time a woman's left buttock as the French actress Micheline Auclair got
out of her bath in *Paris We Love You*. I think I
may say with some pride that even working within
the stifling confines of the industry I have been
able to break new fields, penetrate old barriers,
push sensuality upon areas undreamed of before."

Passion had begun to confuse Murray's command of cliché but not for the world would I have
mocked him. As always, I was spellbound by the
speech he makes me every time we meet; the same
speech yet always with some new detail (Micheline
Auclair's left buttock this time) to ponder, some
act of courage which gained for Murray his lonely
eminence in a hopeless desert of Mayers and
Zanucks.

"But," and his voice became rabbinical in its
solemnity, "in no Murray Morris picture past, present or future will a Greek fuck his own sister."

"Half sister." I tried to sound reasonable.

"You are killing me. I can't make this picture.
Nobody can make this picture."

"Well, you don't have to show them actually
fuck . . ."

"You bet you don't! It would never be shown
anyplacc outside Bel Air where the blue movies are
so popular among my industry friends."

"Maybe if she just says that she is pregnant
. . ."

"By her half brother? Maybe you make her half
pregnant, is better?" There is a Jewish comedian
locked inside the artist bosom of Murray Morris.

"I suppose we can change that."

"*Suppose*, he says!" Murray addressed an imaginary gathering of the Screenwriters Guild. "It

must all go. We begin again. I see a different opening shot. A beautiful pool. With orchids floating
in it. This is color remember and an important
budget. The two sisters are together, bathing, surrounded by their slaves, all girls naturally and not
so good-looking as Lana and Ava but still sexy.
Then there is happy dialogue. We see how the
sisters love each other. Suddenly a man approaches. The girls are at first upset. After all they
don't wear swimsuits. But the man is a eunuch,
and works around the harem."

"How do you explain that to the audience?"

"Lana says to Ava, 'Don't be frightened, dear, it's
only the eunuch who works for me,' or something
like that. Remember, baby, I am *not* writing dialogue. It's just spitballing off the tops of our heads."

We spitballed for a couple of hours, and the
script was left in ruins. I don't know what to do.
I don't think it's possible for me to write the kind
of shit Murray has wanted all along but managed
to disguise by intimidating references to Aristotle
and Dante. He talks like Eisenstein, and thinks
like de Mille.

Anyway I now know about Hollywood, and it's
all true, everything we've ever heard. I have a
strong desire to pack up my camera and head for
Africa or someplace and just take pictures—after
first collecting my money from Murray which is
going to take some doing.

Meanwhile I am again invited to take a crack
at the script. If nothing else, I am learning du-
plicity. I have agreed to make the movie he has in
his head, a saga of courage and passion, of lust
and love . . . you really have to be born for this
kind of thing. It can't be faked. Lesson one for Eric.

A funny moment as I was leaving. "What is this thing you've got about the guy and his sister?" Murray's pig eyes were watery with interest—they are pig eyes, too, with lashes that splay out and up rather than down.

"It just seemed like an interesting relationship." I put on what V. calls my corrupt choir boy face.

"Does Erika know what you've written?"

"What has it got to do with her?" I played idiot boy, and drove Murray wild. He is dying to ask about us but I never give him the opportunity.

So I left after a short, sharp discussion about money. I will be paid next week, he told me solemnly, though he is disappointed in me since he had always thought of me as his creative partner and not just some Hollywood hack.

I came back to the hotel to find your letter. Naturally, I don't want you to marry Benson. On the other hand, I don't want to hear years from now how I ruined your life, that I always dominated you and so on when what I want is the best for both of us. I am having dinner with V. and Tennessee in St. Germain.

NOW

What evening was that? No memory. I sometimes wonder if there is such a thing as the past. Perhaps it is all an illusion, a set of false impressions dealing with possibilities rather than with actual things.

That summer I thought so much about going to bed with Eric that my memory of him, finally, is entirely sensual which is why I have such difficulty in recognizing the author of the red notebook as anyone I ever knew. But then I did not know *him*, only the dream I had of him, an erotic fantasy never translated into actual life because of shyness—no, not shyness, pride. Neither of us would make the first move and so I took another turning; abandoned Eric as unfinished business, now quite finished.

Yet for a long time I enjoyed sentimentalizing what might have been; although to be precise, I knew even then that the Marietta cult of love was not for me. Invariably my interest wanes as my partner's increases and, alas, the other way around. In this at least, Eric and I were alike, and who deserts first would have been our game, a fierce duel if prolonged for there is nothing so brutal as a contest of similar masculine wills. Yet what, paradoxically, makes impossible a long knowledge of one another adds extraordinarily to the excitement of the brief coupling. In fact, I have found nothing to compare to those moments when two bodies separate themselves entirely from personality in that kind of beautiful war which D. H. Lawrence dreamed of but could not bring himself to start, much less win, as he so sadly confesses at the end of *Women in Love* where he finds himself wanting not only the woman but the man, too, and fails to possess either in a way he would like.

Some years ago Lawrence's old patron Mabel Dodge Luhan began to write me letters from Taos (she had found *The Judgment of Paris* Lorenzian). I wrote her back, asked about Lawrence whom I had read with delight at twenty and with disgust, may I say, at forty. She told me that Lawrence had admitted to once having had an affair with a farmer (Lady Chatterley, *c'est lui?*), but nothing lasting came of it—which of course is the whole point: although the male encounter is no more permanent than a flash of lightning, that does not rob it of meaning. Thirty minutes with Eric might have been better than thirty years with Erika. But I made my choice that summer. The mystery continues.

Just as I was about to return to the red notebook, the doorbell rang and there was Fryer Andrews, older and grayer than when I last saw him, and a good deal soberer.

"I have given up drink entirely," he said, stumbling onto the terrace. "The day after New Year's, the doctor took my liver in his hand like this." He opened fingers wide enough to hold a football, then grimly he shut them slowly, wincing with remembered pain. "If you don't want a horrible and painful death never drink again, and I haven't."

Fryer looked as if he might weep. But literary gossip soon recalled him. *The New York Review of Books* did too little for literature (that is, his poetry) and too much for the dizzier aspects of the New Left. Yet of the two of us, Fryer likes anarchy better than I do and regrets his current poet-in-residency at a minor college where the action has been less vivid than at Berkeley or Columbia.

We discussed absent friends, applying to them the same high standards we knew that they applied to us; none measured up. I tend to forget in my Roman life just how bracing the malice of the literary world is and I always look forward to Fryer's occasional visits which usually take place in midsummer when wife and children are abandoned at Sag Harbor so that he can begin touring Europe in a rented car, on the lookout for that perfect seaside resort where he will be able to finish the long poem begun just before the Second War, a work considered by those who have seen its parts (the whole exists only in Fryer's or perhaps Plato's

mind) to be far superior to anything by Auden or
Lowell. But mosquitoes, noise, bad food . . . there is
always something to drive him on to the next town, his
madonna of the future still incomplete but for a perfect hand, the curve of a breast, the beginning of a
smile. Meanwhile when he is not a poet-in-residence, he
teaches English; he taught Eric.

"I haven't thought of him in years. Where is he?"

"Dead." I told him Marietta's story. He was deflected
not by death (Fryer is sixty-four with an enlarged
liver) but by Marietta. "I've never understood your
liking for that woman."

I wearily explained. He did not listen. "She is purest
chloroform. She has given self-love a bad name."

"We've not made it exactly attractive." Despite a
creased magenta face and an enormous stomach, Fryer
considers himself a man of considerable attractiveness
and, it must be granted, women are often beguiled by
his caressing voice and special fame, particularly on the
campuses. In the drawing room, however, he does less
well and of course it is there—perversely—that he most
wishes to glitter. Unfortunately the Duchess of Wind-
sor does not respond to the greenhouse imagery of
Theodore Roethke while Cal Lowell's butchering of
Racine's text is a matter of no great urgency to Madame
Onassis. Yet Fryer is fatally drawn to the company of
the gilded and to the extent he is able, he makes the
rounds like some Californian Proust, mystifying those
who prefer to talk of clothes to even the wittiest bad
news from the world of letters.

"I've often thought you and Marietta were rather
alike." Fryer began to purr as he always does when he
is about to be slanderous. "The two narcissi of the
Forties . . ."

"But still at it, Fryer, and you must admit that after

forty narcissism requires a strong character, hard work . . ."

"All those exercises you do!" With affection, Fryer caressed his stomach's fine parabola which begins almost at the breastbone and finishes well over the crotch. "You're crazy. Women don't care what we look like, and boys only want our money. So why not relax?" He blinked. The word "boy" reminded him of Eric. "I expected him to be enormously successful."

"At films?"

"At anything. He had that awful drive—you had it too when you were his age. Remember our first meeting?" It is a sign of age in Fryer that whenever we now meet certain stories must be retold. This one is never omitted.

I was in uniform, just back from overseas. With a Modern Library edition of Pepys under my arm, I wandered into Times Square's Astor Bar (now torn down), a long dark room filled with soldiers, marines, sailors, and the men who wanted to pick them up, not realizing that the young were there—the world was innocent then —not to hustle but to meet one another. As I approached the bar, a quiet voice quoted, " 'And so to bed.' "

We never did go to bed but over the years we have continued to be friends until I realized quite recently (I am slow in these matters) that Fryer dislikes me; carefully examining myself, I find that my original liking for him has been succeeded by that watchful neutrality with which one tends to look upon the world (had he sensed this in me before I did?). In any case, knowing one another gives neither pleasure. Or as Evelyn Waugh noted, with the passing of time old friendships simply stop, new ones do not start and, finally, there is nothing left but the writer remembering—or in my case trying to remember.

Fryer finished the story of our first meeting some-what perfunctorily, as though he was as tired of know-ing me for so many years as I was of knowing him. Yet I am somewhat annoyed since my lack of interest in him I take to be entirely natural while his lack of in-terest in me betrays bad character.

"Eric was in my American poetry class. He was ridic-ulously attractive. Everyone lusted for him, even my wife—you never met Dagmar, did you? We were di-vorced around then, though not because of Eric. You know she died last year. Everyone died last year. I sometimes think I did, too. I can pinpoint the exact moment of my own death. It was at that party in Princeton where . . ."

Fryer's conversation becomes more Jamesian with each passing year, one thing forever suggesting an-other. But I got him back to Eric, only to have him ask, "Why are you so interested in him?"

I was not prepared to answer (why indeed am I? to recapture my own youth?) and so preferred to speak of Marietta and the screenplay, losing his interest.

Fryer yawned. "There *was* something impressive about him, no doubt of that. He was one of those peo-ple you tend to look at, and not because he was as lovely as his sister. I could hardly keep my hands off her when she came up for the winter dance, and what a scandal that would have been my first year in merry Hanover! I always felt he would do something un-usual in the world."

"Poetry?"

"Oh, no. No talent at all though he did know how to read. He could command a printed page, a lost art." Fryer quoted McLuhan for a time, then: "I don't know what I thought he'd do. A politician perhaps, though

I didn't think that then. But looking back, he was very much in the new style, the Kennedy sort of thing. And the family was rich. Did you know them?"

"Only Erika, the twin sister you lusted after."

"What's she called now, *la duchesse de quelque chose*?" Any reference to a title makes Fryer smile involuntarily, like a carnivore catching the scent of some herbivorous beast.

"Duchesse de Briançon. The Duc has a harelip and sells insurance. They live in Neuilly. I saw her last summer at the Windsors."

This was not true (I had met her at a banker's house in Versailles), but I knew the reference to the Windsors would wound Fryer. It did. He shut his eyes with pain; then rallied. "I had a long conversation about you with one of your alleged relatives, Madame Onassis."

"Not by me alleged." For some years the press has enjoyed relating me to the *ci-devant* tragic empress of the West (yes, Eric's screenplay provides analogies) because my onetime stepfather is currently Jackie's stepfather, a fragile connection which snapped entirely some years ago during a dispute over the late Senator from New York. She liked him; I did not.

I was ready—in fact, waiting—for Fryer to bring up the subject. Not surprisingly, the tragic empress had been appalled by a complete stranger making himself so quickly at home with her. She promptly told a mutual sister who told me.

Happily, I repeated to Fryer some of the things he had said about me. He looked depressed. He has made it a life's goal to establish as fact that I never knew America's holy family. When I asked his present wife why he was so obsessed, she said, "Because that's *his* fantasy life, imagining the great bores of our time are his friends. The fact that you actually know them kills him. But then," she is a long-suffering woman who has learned to hate deeply, "you are *urbane.*"

Fryer dropped the subject for another day. "Eric's family were quite overpowering. I met them all while he was at Dartmouth, and kept in touch with them over the years. They all expected him to be remarkable . . ."

"But he was, in his way."

"Films?" Unlike so many intellectuals, Fryer has not succumbed to the pop arts. For him rock is something the cradle endlessly does while the cinema is a pleasantly trashy complement to the popular novel.

"Yes. Films. He won prizes, for what that's worth. And he did exactly what he wanted to do, which strikes me as a proper life."

"He was certainly vain. No doubt of that. But . . . unsatisfactory." That was to be Fryer's last word on the subject.

We spoke of my sister whom he had seen in Washington when he spoke at the Library of Congress on poetry in the age of science. "No one could hear a word I said." He was very pleased. "The machine broke down."

Would she ever finish the vast historical work she had undertaken? I thought she would. Fryer thought not but then faith in others is not his style. "But she is disturbingly handsome, isn't she?"

We both agreed that not only was she handsome but that she has had a great deal to bear. As if being my sister was not sufficient burden, she is also stepsister to the two most successful adventuresses of our time. For someone with a virtuous (in the ancient sense) disposition to be associated with that never-ending soap opera is a curious punishment. She is also the heroine of a droll revision of the Cinderella story: the two wicked stepsisters move in and take over Cinderella's house; then one marries Prince Charming and the other marries a second Prince Charming, leaving Cinderella to settle down to a quiet life with a good citizen.

"You know whom I also met in Washington . . . Erika's son. What's he called?"

"Eric Benson."

"By her first husband. Yes. He was at my lecture. He's going to Georgetown, studying to be a diplomat."

"How did he strike you?"

"Not as beautiful as his mother, but pleasant looking."

I counted mentally. "He must be twenty-one now."

"Whatever. He graduated from Yale last year. Oh, those Ivy League colleges!" Fryer railed against the colleges where he had once worshipped. Apparently a recent term spent at Berkeley "radicalized" him, to use the latest word. He now favors black power, captive deans, apocalyptic rhetoric.

As usual, I go him one further. I favor the conversion of the universities to temples of Play where forced competitiveness is eliminated and natural competitiveness encouraged; where the worship of work—something hardly anyone does in our vast Affluency (work that is, not worship)—would be discouraged. Within this multiversity would be many mansions devoted, variously, to the saying of Om, to books, to drugs, to sex, to sport and—most important—to warfare. In vast stadia the young would be allowed to fulfill themselves in a series of battles with real blood and real death (only for those who want to play of course—a majority, I suspect, since ours is a violent race). I was eloquent. Fryer did not listen, convinced that I was joking.

"The police are pigs," he said thoughtfully, gazing

171

inwardly at some final battle between *them* and *us*.

"So are the faculty, the students, you and I . . . ours is a porcine race rooting amongst the stars, if I may be poetic." This was the day men circled the moon, preparatory for landing.

"The astronauts!" Fryer snorted, piggishly. "Rotarians in outer space. Could I come by tomorrow? I've met someone you would like."

"Of course," I said, meaning don't.

"An old lady I met on the train from Venice." Fryer smiled happily. "She is a Randolph from Virginia, and knew Eliot in London."

THEN

Tennessee and V. in a long not very interesting wrangle about sex in literature . . . and God knows they ought to be experts. *The City and the Pillar* did wonders for belly-rubbing while *A Streetcar Named Desire* made nymphomania sympathetic: "We've had this date from the beginning."

Tennessee said that though he worked out of sexual obsession, could not in fact get interested in a protagonist unless he was sexually aroused by a character or situation, the use of sex in his work was not an end but a means to "raise the temperature of the audience. You key them up. Then you can tell them anything you like."

"But tell them *what?*" V. is as sharp about the motives of others as he is evasive about his own.

Tennessee was not annoyed. He just chuckles nervously whenever V. is on the attack. "About illusion, I suppose. That's what *Streetcar* is about. Some people, maybe most people, can only live by illusion, and the cruelest thing in the world is

to deprive them of those illusions, which is what
Stanley does to Blanche."

"But then you cast Brando to play Stanley and
he gets the audience's sympathy at the expense of
Blanche. So reality wins."

"Well, there was a certain imbalance in the ultimate production." Tennessee often talks like his
plays, a fine Southern rhetoric, sometimes very
funny. On the other hand, V. talks a great deal
better than he writes. I can never connect him
with that dumb bunny hero of *The City and the
Pillar*.

NOW

A slight chill as I read this. I meant Jim Willard to
be a dumb bunny but . . .

THEN

V. spoke in favor of reality. He thinks that if
people know the worst they can manage to over-
come it or live with it or something.

Tennessee disagreed. "Our illusions are all we
have, any of us."

To which V. answered, "Well, my illusion is that
I am realistic," making a joke of it. I suspect
neither one is right. Most people are both. At least
I am, as you know . . . and aren't yourself. You're
much more like Blanche: what ought to be true
is true.

Then V. needled Tennessee about his excessive
use of sex on stage, and Tennessee countered with
the plot of *Oedipus* in which almost every sexual
tabu held sacred by the audience was violated,
raising their heat in order to show fate working at

the expense of a perfectly nice Theban administra-
tor who was tricked by the gods into marrying his
mother, and so on.

V. agreed that writers have often done this but
made the point that they had to choose carefully
their shock effects because sexual morality is now
changing so rapidly that they are apt to end up
with some ludicrous effect like "Boy died for pu-
rity," a quotation from a book called *The Green Hat*
which apparently made everybody in the Twenties
come but now sounds pretty silly.

NOW

I thought my "theory" about the uses of sexual
shock in art did not occur to me until much later.
Strange to find that I was thinking about it even then.
Obviously one has no new thoughts.

Five years ago at a performance of *A Streetcar
Named Desire* the audience laughed when Blanche described having discovered her young husband in bed
with a *man*, and how he subsequently shot himself.
Today's dramatist would have had the young husband
shoot Blanche, or at least ask her why didn't she
knock? where was she brought up, in a barn?

Nowadays *The City and the Pillar* is about as shock-
ing as a Galsworthy novel. But then I was not "using"
sex to make an effect as much as demonstrating sex of
a certain kind to establish its naturalness in the face of
tribal tabu, a tabu which serenely continues to this day
in the land of the free. When the rewritten version of
The City and the Pillar was brought out a few years
ago, I was startled to find that the popular press was
quite as horrified by the subject as it was twenty years
ago. As our country's first serious novelist, Nathaniel
Hawthorne, said: "The United States are fit for many

174

purposes but not to live in." To which the country's last novelist can only add "amen."

THEN

All in all a pleasant evening, ending up at the Café Flore where all the girls are imitating Juliette Greco including Juliette Greco who was there and all the boys smell to high heaven. Yesterday I went to the Bain de Ligny for the first time to swim and the black toes of France sent me out of there like a shot.

Maybe we Americans, as they say, are sterile, antiseptic, dehumanized and all that but, God, the French are rotting in their clothes. The second I get home with a girl, I point sternly to the bathtub behind the curtain in my room. Gloomily they tidy up, but at least they are used to douching unlike the English. "But it gives you colds!" dipthonged one lovely Cockney, rosy lips bright with fever blisters, proving that you can pick up a cold without washing you know what. V. says the French boys are bearable if you make them keep their shoes on. From the point of view of smell, François Villon would be quite at home around St. Germain but then, as one young existentialist said last night, "France is an old country, unchanging, tired, finished."

Well, I am tired and finished, too—with Murray Morris—finished, that is to say, when I get my money. I've just about run out of Marietta's gift (that's what we gigolos call it) and I don't want to write the family or you (*this is not a hint*).

NOW

I put down the notebook.

Though daylight, I can see the moon, a Shakespearean "gibbous moon." As I watch, three astronauts are going into orbit about it.

Will future generations ever realize the complexity of our response? On the one hand genuine wonder and delight that we are now free of the planet we have spoiled; on the other, the moral numbness that the age of science has somehow managed to instill. It is marvelous, and so what?

They will put up the American flag. They will talk about colonization. They will go to Mars and the outer planets, inhospitable rocks in themselves but eventual stepping-stones to other systems where we can begin to seed with life new worlds, destroying all other forms of life in the process as we have done in our fierce autochthonous way with this poor parent earth.

It is not possible to regard our race with anything but alarm. Yet the tribe-worshippers who make up the majority of mankind take delight in our predatoriness: that's how we made it! From primeval ooze to the stars, we killed everything that stood in our way, including one another. Various religionists have tried to soften or at least disguise our nature but the softening has had no effect while the disguise has never been able to trick for long the eye of the shrewd. I suspect this is why the monstrous self-praise that our race indulges in is so relentless and never ceasing. Every day we are told that man is the supreme work of nature, made in God's image, master of all he surveys, now about to begin the exploration of space—no, not exploration, "conquest" is the word the press uses and for once they are quite right. War is our natural state with one another, with environment, with space, with other worlds where live—what else?—formidable beings whom we must eliminate.

Listening to this ever-increasing roar of tribe-worship, I find myself longing for a sudden sunburst or shift in the magnetic pole, just long enough to remove earth's protective shield and cleanse the planet of its virus, us, or better yet, cause useful mutancies. But one is a part of it all. There is nothing to be done. No way out this side of death. We cannot change, despite the exhortation of the religionists who think that when they say we are nothing before the lord mean only that we are nothing before the idea of our tribal self. Man is his own creator, and may not find meaning outside his own skull. For many of us the importance of art was simply a way of containing the savage thrust of our nature, *making* as best we could rather than destroying. But even art is now sick with blood-longing.

Eric's amateur screenplay demonstrates the passion for domination we all have and never learn to yield with grace. What are Herostratus, Helena and Artemisa but a trinity of self-worshippers, wanting not to give up their identity before the only enemy who has the power entirely to undo them, death, and of the three Herostratus "wins" by burning a building and Artemisa comes in second by building the Mausoleum.

What have the rest of us to show? Eric covered miles of film with pictures. I leave pages marked with black ink, memorials to a dying written culture which does not matter much even now. But then, in Panglossian mood, one tells oneself that what is done from moment to moment is all there is. Life is the present. Nothing more.

I am reminded of a line from that least sympathetic of saints, Augustine (yes, I just looked it up): "In the sojourning of this carnal life each man carries his own heart and every heart is closed to every other heart." In this at least I have more in common with the saint than I have with Tennessee who would argue that the *illusion* that one's heart is open to another's is love enough in our meagre world. Perhaps. But the reality still remains and is the cause of our separateness, our vanity, and our despair.

THEN

Your letter came this morning. Madame Paternault sent it up with the maid who brings me my crust of bread and that peculiar chicory coffee I've begun to like.

Congratulations.

What else can I say? That you did the right thing in marrying Benson? I suppose you did. Anyway it's done, so let's make the best of it as they say, as I guess *I* say, dog in the manger because I never wanted you to marry anyone. That's obvious, isn't it? And stupid, because you had no choice. V. was not about to marry you.

NOW

This is the part I have been dreading. I put down the red notebook, and curse Marietta. How like her to force me to think of these things! For a moment I wonder whether or not *she* is the author of the red notebook composed to . . . to what? That is the question. She is not, finally, malicious, only self-serving and clumsy.

Bastille Day 1948. Erika wears a gray, gauzy evening dress. Everyone stares; she is the queen of St. Germain. Eric is drunk on champagne, and very happy. I drink not at all. Fireworks on the Eiffel Tower. Dancing in the streets. Then just before dawn. . . . No.

There are certain things I have managed with some success to forget or at least not think of and that night is one. Even now memory takes another turning.

I think of the last time I saw Erika. It was shortly

after the Events of May, as the French press likes to refer to the unexpected revolt of the students against the general boredom of their lives. Of those at the lunch, I was the only one who felt that the Events of May had ended unhappily. It is my fate—choice, to be precise—to spend far too much time with those whose political and class interests are the reverse of my own. I daresay this is a kind of recidivism which grows more marked with age. I find restful the wicked and the grand in whose houses I was brought up and though I fled them early, I still return from time to time, pretending that my presence unsettles the magnates when indeed I am at best comic relief so great is their confidence in their rich world.

Erika came toward me. We had not met in fifteen years. Neither smiled. Her face had softened but not aged; and though she was dressed in whatever was currently high fashion she looked to me to be not much different from the Erika I had known at the Hôtel de l'Université.

All about us a green June day, and the sort of people a wealthy host with a famous chef can assemble on a Sunday: exiled royalty, Greek shipowners, dressmakers, ambassadors home on leave and expensive hustlers of both sexes up for sale.

"I've become a Roman Catholic." She chose to begin with a declarative sentence.

"And I was going to say, hello, how are you?"

"I'm quite serious."

"So was I. You look . . . no different."

"I would like to be a nun but I haven't the vocation, and it wouldn't be fair to Hervé." She pointed out her new husband, a Frenchman of the prewar style which seems now to have vanished: parrot-nose, green skin, sunken chest, twig-like limbs, Legion of Honor in

179

lapel. "He looks very . . . French." Conversationally, I did not shine.

"Naturally he wanted me to marry him in the Church and I said I would but now I'm very serious about the whole thing."

"It must fill a void."

"It saved my life, not to mention soul."

"Where is Mr. Benson?" I preferred not to gossip about God at a party to which he had plainly not been invited.

At last she smiled. I had expected a frown. Suddenly I saw Eric's face, too, in the clear blue eyes. "Oh, Benson's very happy. He has a ranch in Canada and a new wife."

The host insisted that I meet a would-be actress who had been the mistress of a recently dead playboy. "You will make her a star," he said to me.

"I am Myra Breckinridge," said the girl quietly, and moved on.

"You're still writing." Erika made it sound a habit not yet given up, like smoking.

"I keep busy. How is Eric?"

"I don't see him."

"Why not?"

But she seemed not to want to answer and so we allowed the host to pull us into a larger group. A Savoia princess spoke of children. A hairdresser spoke of the students and their threat to *us*. The black flag of anarchy had briefly been raised and all had known fear for if the state collapsed who would see to it that the Belon oysters were gathered and brought to Versailles for our lunch?

Rather than make a speech (this was a season of speeches even at lunch parties), I turned back to Erika. "Do you ever see Marietta?"

"I don't read much." Erika has always had a tendency to answer not the question asked but a later one in the same suit.

"Neither do I." This is not quite true. I read a great deal of history, slowly, too many periodicals rapidly, and novels hardly at all. My attention span is not what it was since the thoughts of middle age are short short thoughts. One grows dreamy, reading, and the eye has a tendency to slip from the relentless line of text to the cool white of the margin, and there bathe indefinitely. Is this true of other writers? If so, they ought not to complain about lack of readers when they themselves would never dream of reading the sort of book they so industriously, perversely write. Out of desperation I have abandoned the usual form in order to deal directly with myself, accepting with a good deal of discomfort the current notion that the facts of a life are far more interesting than any work of imagination. Yet I find the process painful and the facts I must now invent most difficult to set down.

We are, I wrote in the film script of *Julian*, what we remember. But what is that? And who are we if memory fails? or even for that matter, as they say, serves?

Remembering Erika last summer in Versailles. The hair is not as dark as it was. Dyed? With most women one would say yes but with Erika perhaps not.

"Marietta keeps on writing." Erika seemed sad at such perversity. "I always thought she was bad for Eric. He was like some sort of . . . fancy man." Where that phrase came from I cannot think.

"You had no other children by Benson?" Dangerous ground. But again she smiled. The teeth were slightly dingy, single flaw in a perfect face, reminding me poignantly of Eric.

"He is at Georgetown University. He wants to go into the diplomatic service."

"He turned out well?"

"I have his picture." She opened her handbag and showed me a snapshot of our son. He was squinting into the sun and I could not tell if he looked like me or not.

Erika used every Christmas to send me the family card with its portrait of herself, Benson and the boy. I always thought this a bit pointed, but was always more pleased than not to see the result of the night we had spent together, Bastille Day, 1948. Also, I am touched at the thought of my flesh continuing even though I do not, for what slight consolation that is, and very slight it is in thoughtful mood since the race will one day—perhaps soon—end entirely and what then will it matter whose seed continued for a time and whose did not? Yet there he was: Eric Benson, a door-prize for attendance, as Dawn Powell used to say.

Had Benson known?

"Well, he knew I was pregnant before we . . . knew each other well." As she put away the photograph I saw a rosary in her handbag, made of cat's eyes.

"That was very good of him."

"Oh, do you think so?" The question was surprisingly blank: do you like Rossini, really?

"Yes. Not many men would . . ."

"Benson was in love with me. At least he wanted very much to marry me. When I told him my situation, what could he do?"

"Tell you to go to hell."

"Oh. I did that on my own." Again the party voice: 'I loved the *Siege of Corinth*.' "He wanted to marry me no matter what, and so he did."

"Did you tell him who the father was?" The question I have wanted to ask for twenty years.

A pause as she took a glass of tomato juice from a waiter. I took a glass of champagne. "He was told, yes."

I was mysteriously disappointed. "And Eric, the boy, does he know?"

"Certainly not. He is Benson's now, in every way."

I revised the will I sometimes write in my head as opposed to the actual one in the safety deposit box. "Then we would not have much to talk about." I cancelled the phantom bequest to my only begotten son.

"No. I should think not."

Benson and Erika had been admirers of Richard Nixon as long ago as 1960. We had nothing in common, except the boy—and Eric. Where was he?

"In Hollywood, making a film, all his own. About long-haired men with beads."

"You sound disapproving."

"Well, it is an odd sort of life."

"Worse than selling insurance in Paris?" I indicated her ducal husband with more disdain than I'd intended.

Briefly Erika's face turned blotchy, pink and white like chintz. Then anger passed, and the non-color returned. "You two are Bohemians—I'm not." I loved her for the word which was almost extinct even in our youth. Yes, she had slipped back in time, a James heroine who had chosen to set up house in a Balzac novel called *La Duchesse de Briançon*, except as luck would have it she was, poor creature, momentarily trapped in *my* novel, and not happy.

She struck back. "You were really in love with Eric, weren't you?"

"Yes," I said. "I was."

"And I was second best that night."

How brutal should truth be? The old debate with Tennessee again. I have mellowed, I suppose. I said, "Not second best. Just something else."

183

"He was in love with you, I think."

I took this revelation as calmly as I could, anesthetized by four glasses of champagne and the June Versailles day. Would I have a vision right now on the terrace like those two English ladies who saw Marie Antoinette and her friends in the woods near the Petit Trianon? Would I see Eric as he was, with my young self beside him, and so much life unlived ahead of us, the two of us pale against the dark green boxwood hedge at the terrace's end? But I saw nothing except our host gently caressing the bottom of the playboy's relic.

"There is no evidence," I said at last. "We played it cool and then we didn't play at all."

"I was so jealous of you."

"I never knew." This was truth.

"Of course not. Because you are insensitive. All you care about is your work, and annoying people . . ."

"*Some* people." This was weak: but then one must always explain, always complain. That is the literary style of our time. "Why should you have been jealous of me?"

But the host was now driving the company toward the dining room and we were separated. I sat between a dressmaker and the girl who was born to play Myra Breckinridge.

THEN

At least Benson is what they call a good provider, and if he goes along with everything then I suppose he's the answer to all our problems but don't count on him always being so complaisant. He's the sort of man to wait twenty years and then suddenly take a knife to you. If it's a boy, name him for me.

V. and I discussed the matter in a setting that I'll

have to wait to tell you about because on the page of even this candid "What I did on my summer vacation" it would seem pretty wild.

NOW

That "wild" scene I remember.

One evening with Cocteau in the Palais Royale, I met an elderly man who had been, Cocteau assured me, Proust's closest friend. I have long since forgotten the best friend's name but he did tell me that Proust had bought a brothel for an Algerian boyfriend and both brothel and Algerian were still in business. On the back of a calling card, he wrote the address of the Hôtel Saumon and the name Said.

I told Eric about this. . . . Why? I suppose to get some sort of clue as to his own behavior, but a brisk "Let's go" was all he said.

On a hot August afternoon we walked through empty streets to the Right Bank (those who have come since cannot realize what a pleasure cities were before the Great Crowding began).

The Hôtel Saumon was in a small arcade just off the square in front of the newspaper *L'Humanité*. It is still there but under different management, and put to less interesting use. That summer was to be the last for Europe's brothels. Communist moralists in France and Italy were already moving to shut down the greatest of human conveniences, filling the streets with girls and boys who spread venereal disease, caused traffic jams and to this day continue to overburden Europe's already inadequate telephone system.

Though Eric and I had, separately, visited some of the more splendid Belle Epoque whorehouses neither of us had ever been to a male brothel. We wondered what it would be like. He pictured something out of

Aubrey Beardsley. I thought it would be like a locker room at the Y. To each his dream.

But the Hôtel Saumon was neither. Just to the right of the front door, beaded curtains separated the dark hall from a small room where Said lay on a sagging divan. He was a powerfully built old man with a bald head which he hastily covered with a red fez as we entered. He gave us a lecherous smile. White slaver was written all over him. I had a vision of Eric in a Saudi Arabian harem being buggered by a sheik. I gave Said the card.

"How good of my old friend to remember me! Sit down. Sit down!"

There was no place to sit but on the divan. Said poured us mint tea which we drank, knowing that it was drugged and we would wake up somewhere back of *outre-more*. But to a Proustian the risk was worth it.

"*He* came here often?" I began.

"Monsieur Marcel? Ah, very often. Yes. He would sit where you are sitting, in the corner, his back to the wall, wearing a fur coat, even in summer, he was always cold, always sick, poor Monsieur Marcel."

But efforts to discover what Monsieur Marcel actually *did* were not directly rewarded. In his way, Said protected the memory of his old patron, telling us no more than that Proust liked to watch others in the act of love through a hole in the wall, a nice symbol since writers are essentially voyeurs, reporting what they have glimpsed out of the eye's corner or overheard at another table, meditating continually upon what others do. How perfectly Beerbohm captured the essence of the novelist when he caricatured Henry James, heavy, formidable, entirely serious, on his knees outside a shut hotel door, studying two pairs of shoes, one male, one female, trying to reconstruct from such meager evidence the two-backed beast within.

As Said talked, facing us on an ottoman, he fondled my right knee and Eric's left knee. "You want a room together?" he asked, not unnaturally I think now but I blushed then.

"No. No."

"Why not?" Eric grinned.

"And old Said could watch through Monsieur Marcel's special mirror." He pinched my knee very hard.

I became dignified. "No. We were simply curious to meet you, having heard so much about you from" (I said the best friend's name) "and then we thought we might, you know, enjoy the establishment."

"You would like a boy?" Said seemed surprised that two young Americans would want to pay.

"Well, yes. I think we would." I turned to Eric who looked less amused than before.

"Good!" Said was all business. "Now you want a boy or a man?" There were, apparently, all sorts of nuances in his profession. *Actif* or *passif* was also most important. To Eric's alarm I described what, I assured Said, was Eric's passion, something powerful, gorilla-like, hugely hung with what the French call a wounding-prick. Eric was by now quite pale, particularly when Said, growing more and more excited at the prospect of serving such an attractive client, declared he had exactly what Eric wanted, an Arab mechanic just arrived from Oran. I put in an order for a boy, non-Arab. Singing loudly in a minor key, Said excused himself and thundered up the rickety stairs.

"That," said Eric, "was a shitty thing to do."

"But you don't have to *do* anything. Just pay him."

"It'll be embarrassing."

"Then why did you want to come?"

"Who wouldn't want to see a boy whorehouse that belonged to Proust." He looked me straight in the eyes. "Why don't we take a room together?"

I shall never know what the look meant, or the question for that matter. In the last twenty years I have put every possible construction on both. I suspect, all in all, it was, as they say now, a put-on. Anyway there is no use speculating. If an opportunity was missed, it was forever missed.

"You'll be happier with the mechanic from Oran." Young men never give one another an opening in their unremitting war for dominance. Though I have often thought that had he actually offered me one that afternoon at Said's, my life might have been (no, not really) changed.

Eric laughed, the invitation, if such it was, not renewed. "The only thing like that I ever liked was in school. He was on the baseball team, too."

"What happened?"

"Killed in the Marine Corps. I never saw him after we were sixteen, seventeen."

"If he'd lived, would you have taken up where you left off?"

"What would be the point? Erika liked him, too."

"You act as a team?"

"Have you noticed that?"

"It's hard not to."

Eric played with the beads of the curtain, made them rattle. "I think we're attracted to the same people. We're twins, after all."

"Same thoughts? Premonitions? Dreams?"

"We often have exactly the same response to people."

"To me?" That took courage, but the divan on which Proust had so often sat made me reckless.

Eric did not entirely answer. "And people often respond to us in the same way. Think I'm Erika, Erika's me."

I grew cold in the stuffy room. Had she told him?

Yes, she had. He was most deliberate. "She's pregnant."

"Since when?" Not the splendid response one would have liked to make.

"She missed her first period two weeks ago, just after she got back."

"I see."

He was expressionless. I would not have expected him to be outraged but, on the other hand, what was a brother to do? and a twin at that with a penchant for the other's friends.

"What do you expect . . ." I started to stammer, something I have seldom done since I left my stepfather's house. He, poor man, had stammered badly and there were those who thought that I was imitating him deliberately when all I had done was respond in much the same way he had to a virago-ridden environment, scatter words, do not concentrate your fire, such are the diversive tactics of the unconscious mind when faced with the unsupportable ". . . want me to do?" I got the sentence out.

"Nothing. What could you do?"

"Marry her."

"You don't want that."

"No. Does she?"

"No."

I was hurt. Is it not always better to reject than be rejected? The twins were winning not only the battle but the war.

Eric suddenly smiled in just the same way Erika had smiled at me the next morning when I woke up with a start to find myself in her bed and not my own. "She's going to marry old Benson. Luckily, he doesn't mind being the father to your child."

"She works . . . rapidly," was all I could say.

"Well, she does have an interest in survival. She'll always do well. Fact, I've been writing about someone just like her, for Murray's movie." But at that time I had not read "The Two Sisters of Ephesus." Which was Erika, Artemisa or Helena? Which, for that matter, was Eric? He did not seem much like Herostratus.

Memory stops, reverts with new interest and pain: what would have happened if I had said yes at the Hôtel Saumon and we had taken a room together?

Said returned. "They are ready for you, *mes gosses*." He then explained that although he had alerted the pair he thought we would like, we were to be shown his entire stock of twelve men and four boys (Said had an Arab precision about these things not easy to grasp). Apparently none lived in the hotel; rather they would wander in, particularly around five o'clock when businessmen would drop by on their way home from office to family.

Up the stairs we went to a room not much larger than the office downstairs. Here, drinking wine and playing cards, were a number of Paris toughs of various ages and origins (one Negro, several Arab). They looked at us with the normal hostility of any male pack faced with strange bucks.

Said introduced us. They stared; we stared. One powerfully built Arab with a scarred face pointed at Eric and grinned at Said who nodded: the mechanic from Oran.

Then we stepped outside and I said I would like a blond youth who, according to Said's strict category, was a man although in America he would have been considered a boy since manhood does not begin for us until at least twenty-five.

The two joined us on the landing. Solemnly, we shook hands. Then the blond and I were shown into a bedroom arranged in Arab style with a divan half-hidden by beaded curtains, ottomans, a brass water pipe and an inlaid ivory table (had Proust done the decorating?), all thick with a half century's dust.

Chuckling happily, Said shut the door as the grave young man filled a basin with water, set it on an ottoman, took off his clothes and without self-consciousness began to wash his haunches, all the while telling me how he was an engineering student from Grenoble who had made the mistake of marrying before he finished his studies, and what with prices the way they were in Paris he and his wife and child would have long since starved to death without Said's establishment.

I could not resist asking did the wife know (how did a nice boy like you get in a business like this?)? He was shocked. Of course not. Wives had quite enough to do without interfering in a man's private life.

Two weeks later I ran into him on the Quai Voltaire. He was pushing a baby carriage; his wife beside him. But since he now wore thick glasses, I don't think he recognized me. In any case, I didn't say hello, respecting his secret life. I did note that the wife looked as if she might be pregnant; in which case she had, unknowingly, condemned her husband to many grim afternoons at Said's.

When we had finished, I paid the young father from Grenoble the agreed on sum (about five dollars for him, I think, and five for Said) and joined Eric downstairs. He was standing, somewhat pale, back to the wall of Said's office, trying to keep Said from kissing him.

"What took you so long?" Eric leapt past Said and joined me at the door, causing the glass beads of the curtains to clatter shrilly.

"So beautiful," Said observed without apology. "He could make a fortune here."

"I bet you say that to every pretty . . . face," Eric almost said "fesse," "that comes in here." Eric was now his usual cool self.

"So few come in here, wanting to pay that is. Now in the old days Monsieur Marcel's friends were often young and charming but not like this, so manly." We left, after many handshakes.

I have since wondered if there were a Madame Said, and young Saids. There is so much now that I would like to know about him but twenty years ago he was simply another gargoyle bursting from the Gothic edifice of my youth—to be looked at with the same degree of interest that one studied Marietta's rose window or the prophets Gide and Santayana to left and right of the west door.

Eric was indignant. "I thought that Algerian would kill me."

"Said?"

"The mechanic. When we got to the room I told him it's all a joke, that this isn't really my sort of thing, you know, the line, but then he grabs me by the neck —I think I've got bruises—and says, 'I have a family. No work. I need money.' So I say, I'm sorry to hear that things are going bad with you, *copain*, and I will pay the tariff whatever it is so don't get all upset. Well, that soothed him and he flashed his gold and silver teeth at me—I felt like telling him if he was so broke he could always sell his mouth—and then I suggested we sit down and talk about Marcel Cerdan and Edith Piaf or baseball or something for a decent length of time and then go downstairs, everybody satisfied. But no. He started in again. He wanted me, he said. He would make me happy. I said I didn't see how that was possible. He said he would try. It would be fun. I said from what I'd heard about Arabs that what would be fun for him would be a pain in the ass for me. He said he was gentle as a gazelle on a mountain peak or something. I understood about every third word. I said I was sure he was but since he was a big strong man and I an innocent little shaver—at Dartmouth mutual masturbation was regarded as going all the way—I couldn't. This was a mistake. The thought I was a virgin drove him wild. He jumped on me. I got away. We rolled around the floor. Then I yelled for help and Said came running in with, so help me, a whip in one hand. God knows what scene he thought he was going to join in but before he could do anything, I said, 'if you don't get this bastard off me I'm going to yell for the police.' That was the end of that. The mechanic joined the other kids in the bullpen and Said took me down to his room to try to find out what was wrong with me."

"A nice experience."

"No." We were now at the Rue de Rivoli with its bullet-gouged arcade. "Do you really like that sort of thing?"

"It saves time." I was deliberately callous. "Each party to the transaction knows what's expected of him. One takes money, one takes pleasure. It's the most civilized of human institutions."

"Not for me."

"You do the same."

"I don't pay."

"You also don't give much, do you?"

Eric looked at me with puzzled dislike. "How would you know what I *do?*"

"We have Marietta in common. Remember?"

He remembered to smile. "Well, that's different. She exploits our—*my* youth at least. You were born middle-aged."

I took this as a compliment though it was not meant to be. "I chose not to be young," I began with the autobiographical intensity of the young person I was.

The young search not for love but for someone they can talk to about themselves or, best of all, to find that most marvelous of creatures who will, without fatigue or apparent boredom, analyze them by the hour. Henry Miller's life quest (according to his books) is setting traps for this rare bird.

Of the disappointments of my own youth, I recall not so much love affairs gone wrong as those moments of intimacy when at last the dominant theme of the duet was clearly myself, when point counterpoint vain youth and admirer were developing the splendid harmonies of my uniqueness and then, like a non-serial dissonance in a usual work, the music went sour and the other made reference not to me but to self. Such betrayals are impossible to forgive.

It is the genius of Marietta that, liking young men, she understands their egotism and so is able to hold in check her own, and talk to them tirelessly about themselves. Thus was I trapped, thus was Eric ensorcelled not to mention Guido, Derek and Benjamin though now, I suspect, money plays a part. If so, she has become that purest of artists, the analyst who pays the patient.

"You didn't think of Erika like that." Before us the empty Place de la Concorde wavered in August heat.

"Like what?" I had been thinking of how I had enlisted in the army at seventeen, gone overseas at eighteen, written a novel at nineteen, become a civilian at twenty when I met Marietta. Prematurely aged, I looked with compassion upon my prep school contemporaries who were putting in time—even as we walked along the Rue de Rivoli—at Harvard while I was in the world. I had told Eric and Erika this story many times, never failing to interest myself with each repetition, and Erika had always listened gravely while Eric waited impatiently for me to pause so that he could discuss *his* escape from the navy (he had gone AWOL the day after the war in Japan ended and only family influence had saved him from prison) and the conventional world of universities, jobs in Wall Street, and nice girls at the Maidstone Club in Easthampton. Only my passion for him (quite vanished, I decided, as we paused in the shade of the Hôtel Crillon) had made me put up with a self-absorption so clearly resembling my own.

"You didn't want to just please yourself and not her, did you?"

"Ask her."

"I will."

So we parted. I returned to the Left Bank and he went on to the Prince des Galles to see Murray Morris.

It is curious but my most vivid impression of Eric is at that moment of parting. I can see him now quite clearly. Blond hair tangled, face flushed in the heat, jacket slung over right shoulder, shirt damp with sweat between the shoulder blades.

That makes two pictures of him: on the floor with the camera at the hotel, and turning from me to walk toward the Champs-Elysées. They are like sections of film which do not vary with replaying. They are also all that I have left of him for I no longer recall his tone of voice or anything else except that I remember once remembering having remembered—a thousand begats

—back to the original moment which I could never begin to recall as it was, only as I thought of it last. We lose our past long before we lose ourselves.

Yet there are unexpected moments of recollection. In Rome whenever I turn down the street which goes past the Hotel Eden where I lived when I first came to Europe after the war, I can sometimes see myself coming up the street, a ghost not knowing he's being watched by me, by a stranger old enough to be his father, and yet the instant we pass one another and I see the same face I look at every day—but as it was then, unlined, pale, intense—time overlaps for an instant and I am he. I know what he is thinking, where he is going, and I can even quote—almost from memory —the lines he wrote that day. (*A Search for the King* was the book and the first lines he wrote, after settling in Rome, were "toward some further mystery time moved, and the days, the moments of light and dark passed, and he moved, like time, toward a mystery he could not name, a place beyond illusion, larger than the moment, enlarged by death.") Then the present intrudes and what I was is gone and what I am is— going.

Contemplating that passage from *A Search for the King* (I just copied it out of a depressing-looking paperback), I wonder what I meant by "mystery." It seems to me now that there is nothing mysterious at all about our lives. They start, flourish, stop. Naturally there are puzzles. I would like to know whether or not the universe is finite or infinite. I would like even better to be assured that the two words are meaningless. But excepting the sort of puzzle which makes our passage here interesting and gives incentive to our questing games, I see no mystery at the heart of things and take comfort from Wittgenstein's profoundly unpopular dictum, "Philosophy simply puts everything before us, and neither explains nor deduces anything. Since everything lies open to view there is nothing to explain. For what is hidden, for example, is of no interest to us." Substitute the word "novel" for "philosophy" and one begins to find a way of showing things, or perhaps simply of confronting things upon the page.

To show my relations with brother and sister is to "explain" everything. But the desire for mystery is deeply human and occurs at every level from those intellectuals who seize on Christ or Marx in order not to assume responsibility for their own works and days to the semiliterates I so often meet in my prowlings who have absolute proof that the whole thing is explained inside the Great Pyramid at Giza or that, more usually, there is this book somewhere they saw once or were told about that has all the answers and if only they could get their hands on it we'd *know* because like it's all in there.

Poor monkey race, wanting so much never to die that life itself is constantly spoiled by a passion for mystery, for the descent into some secret cellar where all is finally explained; the price of this knowledge (and continuation) involving no more than a small sacrifice to the cellar god: the surrender of reason and the ritual letting of blood.

THEN

After I left V., I went to see Murray at the hotel. With him was a plump little man with damp paws and thick glasses. "This," said Murray proudly, "is Clyde R. Bannister Jr."

I must've looked puzzled.

"Baby, *Clyde R. Bannister Jr,* the screenwriter."

I remembered: "The Two Sisters of Ephesus, a

treatment by Murray Morris and Clyde R. Bannister Jr." So Mr. Bannister, last referred to as "a fink" was on the scene again.

"I don't have to tell you Clyde's credits. He works with Mike Curtiz, my old friend, when he does not work for Murray Morris."

"That's quite a script you've written there, Eric," said Clyde.

"Thanks, Clyde." I said his name clearly in true Hollywood fashion.

"Clyde here," Murray moved his cigar at Clyde to make absolutely certain that I knew who he was. Ash dropped on Clyde's knee. He smiled at Murray.

"Sorry, baby." Murray dusted the knee with a napkin already thick with what looked to be mayonnaise from the lobster on the table. Mayonnaise and ash made a nice little mess on Clyde's knee. Clyde gave Murray a look of doglike devotion.

Murray looked at what he had wrought and decided to ignore it or, as they say in show business, "If you lay an egg, step away from it." "Clyde's been traveling in Europe with Betty Lou his wife, a wonderful girl . . ."

"She's devoted to you, too, Murray . . ."

"And when he heard I was here, dropped by for the old time's sake . . ."

"That's right, Murray."

". . . so I felt obligated morally to show him our script and what you had done, Eric. He hasn't seen your movie which was at Cannes . . ."

"But I hear good things about it, Eric. Really good things."

It was like the time I smoked opium at the hotel with what's his name, and after just one drag on that long wooden pipe I started to float away, a strange sensation because I knew who and where I was and why I seemed to be floating but I couldn't stop the sensation. Well, that is what Murray and Clyde were doing to me. From miles away I heard them droning.

"Clyde's structure-sense is first-rate . . ."

"Murray's understanding of character is profound . . ."

"Clyde feels he can make a contribution . . ."

"With Murray's sense of audience, he knows how to excite an audience, but always in good taste . . ."

"Clyde's worried about the shape of the story . . ."

"Murray knows how I work. You see, Eric, there's got to be a beginning, middle and an end. All great writers work that way. Take W. Somerset Maugham . . ."

I rallied. "Or take Franz Werfel."

Murray gave me a suspicious look. He knows I am sometimes prone to "destructive sarcasm." "Yes, Eric. Franz would not be found dead if one of his classics did not have a beginning, middle and an end."

"So what's on your minds, men?" I became Dartmouth-hearty.

"Baby, if I have said it once I have said it a thousand times, you are a natural, filled with talent . . ."

"A really first-rate first draft, Eric . . ."

"Yes, first-rate for the first time writing an A movie for major world release. But as you know there has been sometimes disagreement between us on concept, like our protagonist fucking his own sister."

"Yes, Eric, that is not really good taste. The Johnston office would never pass it . . ."

"But even if they would what has that to do with the rivalry of two wonderful fun-loving girls, and believe me, baby, you must—the audience must *love* these girls . . ."

"We must have empathy for them, Eric."

"Well, baby, I ask you how can anyone have empathy for the two cunts you have written about?"

"But I don't think they are cunts. I think they're . . . normal." I had used the wrong word. I was also on the wrong tack. Never defend in Hollywood-land—attack! I was lost.

Murray turned to Clyde, his face a mask of horror. "Normal! Clyde, he says they are *normal!*"

"I must say I don't think it's normal to go to bed with your brother. No, I don't."

"But a natural thing to *want* to do." I kept trying.

"Baby, you're trying to shock Clyde. Clyde, he lives in the same hotel as Tennessee Williams. He tries to imitate him."

"A sick mind, Tennessee Williams." Clyde looked deeply troubled. "I'm surprised, Eric, that you would want to have anything to do with such a sick person."

"Oh, God." I began but Clyde was reminiscing. "You know, Murray, I met Tennessee at Metro when he was working on *Marriage Is a Private Affair*, a nice fellow I thought but then when I saw *Streetcar* last winter I said to Betty Lou, 'This is not a healthy mind.' But some of his dialogue for *Marriage* was A one."

I was worked over. No one fucks his sister and if he does you can't tell an audience because they won't stand for it. As good a reason for staying away from audiences as any I have heard lately. My girls are insufficiently fun-loving.

"I see them," said Murray grabbing his balls thoughtfully, "*bathing* together."

"A good opening scene, Murray." Clyde was nodding with discovery and pleasure.

Anyway Clyde has agreed to do his version of my version based on his treatment (with M.M.) of the 2 S's of E, and then "Baby, all three of us will work together, a happy family because . . ." Eyes gleaming with pleasure at the thought, he munched the undercarriage of an already viscerated lobster. "Norman Z. McLeod is interested, according to his agent, very interested."

"I like Norman," said Clyde, "a fine moviemaker."

"Who," I asked, "is Norman Z. McLeod?"

Pity mingled with contempt in four magnified eyes. "Just the director of one of your biggest hits from Goldwyn last year . . ."

"*The Secret Life of Walter Mitty*, Eric, with Danny Kaye . . ."

"I hated it." I did, too.

"Domestically it will gross four million easy." The aesthetics no longer seem of much concern to Murray. More to the point, what small hope I might have had of directing the picture could now be officially abandoned. I can't say I was very happy but I played along with the monsters. It is now agreed that I will stand by while Clyde takes "a crack at" the script. Then we will all sit down together and "kick it around."

Finally, with the courage of disaster, I said to Murray, "When am I going to be paid?"

"Paid?" The word was obviously new to him but

he was willing to learn it; after all, he has a gift for languages and can speak nine, with an accent. "Paid?" He has now figured out the meaning from the context. "Baby, your check was mailed last week to your hotel."

"I never got it."

"But I saw my secretary put it in an envelope and . . . Well, we shall look into this. Yolande!" The bedroom door opened and a girl struck a Folies-Bergère attitude, wearing only panties.

"Is this the secretary?"

"For God's sake, Yolande, put on your clothes! She was bathing, baby. Such a hot day. Eric tells me, Yolande, you did not mail the letter to the Hôtel de l'Université."

"I did not? Or I did?" She began to giggle; no one had given her this script and she was bad at improvisation.

Murray turned to me. "She is usually a most efficient secretary. Anyway I shall personally see that a messenger brings you the check tomorrow." He gestured at the girl who still stood, posing in the doorway, waiting for cue lines. "Yolande, please put some clothes on, and finish that—uh, typing I gave you."

Yolande vanished but left the door open. Inside I could see a second girl lying on the bed, also undressed. Murray was up to his old tricks.

"I'll take the check now." I was firm. Clyde pretended he was not in the room, obviously his lifework.

"Baby," Murray began. Then he stopped, aware that for once I meant business. Without a word, he marched to the desk, and wrote out a check for one thousand dollars and gave it to me.

"But that's not what we agreed on. . . ." I was set for a row, pleased that Clyde R. Bannister Jr was in the room, adding to Murray's embarrassment.

"Eric!" Murray was breathing heavily, face mottled with fury. "You have not yet met the requirements of our agreement and done a complete screenplay with *two* rewrites. You cannot receive the full amount under the Screenwriters Guild. Am I right, Clyde?"

Clyde cleared his throat, like a toilet flushing, and said yes.

"Anyway we talk in a few days, once Clyde has got the feel of the material."

I gave up. After all, a thousand dollars is better than the nothing he had intended me to have. As I rose to go, Yolande and her girl friend came to the bedroom door to see me off. The friend blew a kiss at Clyde who waved vaguely with three fingers like Hugh Herbert.

"Nice to meet you, Clyde," I said giving him a firm handshake. Then I turned to the second girl in the doorway. "And you, too, Betty Lou." On that high note I left.

NOW

The sun has set behind St. Peter's. The low-swarming birds are gone. In the west cobalt blue has become neon rose. The moon's dead face reflects the now hidden sun.

I am depressed, partly at time's passage (how did one get so quickly from there to here?), partly at Eric's description of a script conference—in just such a way I once earned my living—and at the glum realization that I forgot to arrange to have sex today. As I write this phrase, I am reminded of a newspaper writer who found distressing my habit of using the phrase "to have sex" instead of "make love." But having sex is a fact and describable, while making love is an illusion and indescribable. I have always thought it wiser and more honest to deal with facts than evoke illusions no matter how self-flattering. Needless to say, one usually does both, but one ought always to try to begin with fact if only to discover exactly where one is.

Where am I? Well, I have gone inside, turned on the lights in the living room, look for comfort to the Amalfitan stone lion which dominates the room (said to be eleventh century, probably stolen from a church), look at the marble head of Jove bought from a dealer now disappeared and wish for the hundredth time that the marble did not so much resemble those Ivory Soap Parthenons I used to carve in the third grade.

The room's yellow walls usually cheer me but not now. The unfinished business of Eric, the never-finished business of Marietta, not to mention a long attack on me which a thoughtful friend sent from London. I have glanced at it. Apparently, I am not as committed, as self-revealing, as powerful as *Mailer*. To which I can only murmur "bullshit." Yet it is strange how our careers seesaw. Ten years ago the English were comparing Mailer unfavorably to me. Whenever I am up, he is down, and the reverse. Currently he is very much up for this is the age of writer as subject, and Norman is a most appealing subject. He looks like everyone his age. He makes social messes which to our pre-pot whiskey drinking generation are chillingly familiar (incidental intelligence: I have known or known about most of the American writers of my time and I can think of only three who are not—or were not once—alcoholics).

Finally, Norman throws himself so whole-heartedly into current events that the fact he invariably sinks like a stone makes no difference, perhaps is the difference. Certainly his Mr. Magoo approach to history is profoundly endearing, and his perennial threat one day to write that Great Novel (oh, lost, lost, and by the *Sunday New York Times Book Section* grieved!) has, with time, become the Great Novel itself. He need do no more; he *is*, until the fashion again changes and he is forgotten with all the rest, good and bad. Personally, we have always got on—the result of a tacit nonaggression pact (though not necessarily one of mutual-assistance); after all, each has distressed so many dominations and powers both political and literary that it would be too much for either to have to endure the other's sniping.

I am smiling, as I write. I always smile when I think of Norman. I recall an evening we spent together in New York, discussing his play version of *The Deer Park*, and drinking a good deal. Then I took him up-town to an apartment where Paul Bowles was staying. Norman had never met Bowles, or Allen Ginsberg (then unbearded) and Peter Orlovsky who were also present. Conscious that literary history might be made, Bowles tried to tape the conversation, but, predictably, we all talked at once and only the sharp cries of a large green parrot were ever entirely clear on the playback.

Suddenly, Norman lay down on the floor and shut his eyes. Putting his feet comfortably on Norman's stomach, Ginsberg said, very kindly, "Of course he's crazy."

But memory plays tricks. Although there is often a parrot present when Bowles is at home, I now have an amending memory that the cries on the tape were not a parrot's but Orlovsky's. Others present will no doubt remember, although I have usually found that whenever I read about an occasion where I was present, the report (except once) never tallies with my own. The once was Jack Kerouac's *The Subterraneans* in which he describes with—to my mind (for what the sieved instrument is worth)—astonishing accuracy an evening he spent with William Burroughs and me. Everything is perfectly recalled until the crucial moment when Jack and I went to bed together at the Chelsea Hotel and, as he told me later, disingenuously, "I forgot." I said he had not. "Well, maybe I wanted to." So much for the tell-it-like-it-is school.

Memoirists, however, are seldom as precise as novelists. I have been reading John Lehmann's autobiography in which he describes our meeting with André Gide. He reports that later I "sighed" because Gide had made no mention of a book I'd sent him when, in actual fact, I had simply wondered if he had ever got the book, not quite the same thing as being disappointed, and all that that implies. Then Lehmann neglects to mention the only interesting thing the Master said. He had just been awarded—to his obvious delight —the Nobel Prize. With a great smile, the deep Comédie Française voice intoned, *"Premier le Kinsey Report, et après ça le Prix Nobel."* He then gave me a copy of *Corydon,* a book which he assured me solemnly he seldom gave anyone. On the flyleaf he wrote *avec la sympathie,* a rather cold dedication according to a knowing French friend.

What else do I remember of Gide? Short, thickchested, with large peasant hands; wearing a dark green velvet jacket, beret, large round spectacles. He sat at a plain work table surrounded by books on two levels; the upper level reached by stairs. Open in front of him (staged for our benefit?) was a pornographic novel by an Anglican priest recently retired to the English countryside. The pages were beautifully hand-printed, and there were a number of drawings of boys being debauched. With a grin, Gide said he had received the manuscript some time ago but had not yet decided how to answer its priestly author.

"*C'est intéressant, maître?*" I asked.

"*Oui. Mais le style, hélas, c'est un petit peu trop littéraire pour moi.*" Impression: a nervous malicious intelligence, not very like the somewhat histrionic self-examiner of the Journals, forever preparing a brief for the defense to be tried in the court of a Protestant god whose jurisdiction the defense must, in all conscience, deny.

Thinking of Gide, I suddenly wonder why it is that so few American writers have ever wanted to appear intelligent. Many of course were—and are—not. But those few who could compare in civilization with their European counterparts chose, protectively, to hide their wit as tribute to Demos. "Ahm just a farmer," drawled Faulkner, while Stephen Spender tells of meeting Hemingway in Spain during the Civil War and listening to him talk intelligently of Stendhal until, realizing that he had been sounding literary and un-American, he quickly reverted to his usual bullying baby talk. Our writers are like city-bred politicians forced through gerrymander to represent rural constituencies.

Part of Norman Mailer's craftiness was to assume early on the Hemingway life-style and manner because it was familiar to the public (and since so little is known to the minority which reads newspapers, an ambitious writer can hardly be faulted for wanting to identify himself with a known archetype like Hemingway, Faulkner, Fitzgerald). Consequently the public has been charmed that the boozing, the brawling, the marrying, all that they have been taught by the press to believe is the necessary behavior of a major writer, continues now in Norman, heir to Papa. Unfortunately, Mailer's intelligence keeps breaking through and one senses that beneath the mask he elects to wear there is a nice Jewish boy (his own phrase) playing desperately at being a Goyisher slob, and hoping that his liver —not to mention nerves—will survive the strain. One wonders what Norman would have been like had he been himself. Faced with much the same problem, Saul Bellow in his first two books tried to write as if traditional English was entirely natural to his ear, then, sensing perhaps that he was playing a part, he shifted ground, began to use his Jewishness to make a language and an art all his own.

Once, to annoy Norman, I asked him why Jewish-American writers wrote such bad prose (most of them do, not that anyone cares). Norman took in stride my crude lumping together. "Because," he said, "they hear such bad English when they're growing up."

Gide thought falsity of tone the one thing fatal to a writer. Yet perhaps it is not possible to survive in a society which hates the examination of anything except machinery without becoming a clown, a monster, a performer willing to play any role in order to reach that vast audience which is the true creator's goal though not, as newspaper writers think (betraying their own interest), for money or glory but for making connection. That is the passion which drives the talent, and the larger the connection the greater the fulfillment.

Examining sales figures with a sharp eye, going into depression at the slightest falling off, Dickens is typical of the artist who finds in the people of his own time the self's true complement. It is perhaps significant that my generation was the last to think of the novelist as central to the culture, with everyone potentially accessible to our art. When this proved not to be true (our medium too "hot"; our readers too "cold"), writers began to act very oddly indeed, running for President, directing films, talking on television.

Fortunately, the rising generation is more modest than we. They know that the novel at its best is for the few, like poetry, and so they are able to survive reasonably content in universities, while we—last of the great dinosaurs—sink into the electronic swamp, our death agonies recorded on television with much fuss.

Beside the review from England, a letter from a Canadian academic saying that the only two characters in literature which no one but an American could have created are Huckleberry Finn and Myra Breckinridge (so much for the white whale!), and a cable from Hollywood: would I like to adapt for the screen Kurt Vonnegut's *Slaughterhouse-Five?* A nice irony. Vonnegut is, the press tells us, the current favorite of the young, supplanting Golding and Salinger and Tolkien. I think I know why. Though his style is easy to the point of being imbecilic, his creative imagination is—what is the reviewer's phrase?—first-rate and fills the need of the young for fantasy, for alternative worlds to this one. Last year they were Tolkien elves, this year they can learn not to fear death because it is simply a violet light and, as creatures from another planet assure us, since one is able to scan one's life at any point, if things are bad in the present simply go backward or forward in time.

It is quite possible that the only fiction that is "necessary" in this time is science fiction. The young want mind-bending stories and—finally—hope of heaven. I have noticed that the one book of mine they read voluntarily is *Messiah*, because it deals with what might be the next world religion and so has the look of science fiction.

Significantly the only dead writer much admired today is Hermann Hesse who is forever journeying to the East, translating Zen for the West, and creating protagonists who are young, troubled, marked in a way that only the initiated can see—and what sensitive young person in a suburb of Cincinnati does not believe that he, too, has been singled out, and finds reassurance in Hesse's pages that there are others—though not too many—like himself?

To serve the solipsism of youth has always been a shortcut to glory. But though Hesse is not as much to my taste as Thomas Mann (no longer read at all as far as I can determine), he was at least authentic and authenticity is the most one can ask of a writer. Certainly lack of authenticity has made most contemporary work unbearable. When William Styron asked me what I thought of the short stories in the first issues of the *Paris Review* I said, unkindly but accurately, "They are rejects from *The Saturday Evening Post*."

At the time I thought it funny—but now think it sad—that after our war so many nicely brought up boys would want, for a time at least, to play at being Artists and start little magazines in Paris, because isn't that what they all did at the end of the First War? Yes, they did. So why not do something else?

Looking back, one can now see that a whole generation set out to imitate an earlier generation, a very strange thing to do—and not just the untalented: even our good writers deliberately put on the masks of their predecessors while those few who chose to be themselves, like John Horne Burns, had a bad time of it. Yet whenever I think of the authentic I think of the clumsy but passionate Burns or the meticulous Paul Bowles creating his own landscape and peopling it with characters never seen before in our literature. One feels that those two needed to do what they did—and for that matter Hesse, Tolkien, Golding are equally authentic and, like them or not, this wholeness is what literature is all about, and something quite remote from all those portentous renderings of The American Experience when wife went to bed with best friend on a campus last summer and, oh, the pain and wonder of being Jewish!

I will not adapt *Slaughterhouse-Five*, I decide, crumpling the cablegram and setting fire to it in an ashtray . . . cleansing fire, as Heraclitus (also of Ephesus) knew.

Why, I suddenly wonder, is the legend of Herostratus so appealing? Because it is the destructive side of the Shakespearean proud boast to make a lover immortal with a line of words? Or is it that we come from fire and shall end in fire when the sun flares, and the universe falls back upon itself, as the cycle of creation prepares to begin again (what a splendid image Calvino makes of this in *Cosmicomics*).

Fire was our beginning and still bemuses us even though we ourselves are a heavier, duller element, oblongs of soft skin containing scarlet seawater held upright by a fibrous contraption more suitable for a vegetable than for such a proud sentiency as man.

Recently I dreamed of my father who died and was cremated last winter. He was seated in some sort of a funicular car moving slowly opposite to me. As we came abreast of one another, I saw with dull horror that he was dead and where his eyes should have been there were bright flames. Ultimate fate of watery creatures in a fiery universe.

THEN

How much should I tell you? I never know. It is harder writing the truth than saying it. But you say you want to know everything I do and think—can't say at the moment there's much of either going on—and so I must tell you that I think a good deal about you and poor Benson, yes, *poor* Benson because once you decide to charm someone you do it entirely and they haven't a chance . . . except I had a chance, didn't I? But it's just as well we're finally on our own. I feel like a Siamese twin who has managed to survive the knife that separates.

There is also something new, just beginning. Perhaps my equivalent of poor Benson.

I am writing this while she sleeps. She is not at all like you, you will be annoyed to know. The sheet is bunched under her chin and she has fallen into the central furrow of my heroic mattress. Dark hair covers the pillow, the strands crossing and crisscrossing as though woven—why, I wonder, all these metaphors?

There is a girl in my bed. Her clothes are on the floor, mixed with mine. I am bare-ass at the table writing this for your amusement (?), as I wait for a call from the bank. I can smell her on me, in fact the mingling of her smell with mine, bottled, would put Chanel out of business.

It began last night when some friends took me to the house of François Reichenbach, a rich, very nervous young Frenchman who is fascinated by Americans (he'll outgrow that) and obsessed by movie-making, like me. He is already beginning to make his own movies, admires my picture, wants to work with me though I suspect this was simply politeness.

All sorts of movie people were present. A few I'd heard of. Most not. Anyway it was pleasant to be around people who are interested in the same things I am though of course the taste of the French *avant-garde* is perverse: they think Howard Hawks is a master, and dislike Pare Lorentz . . . and if you try to say a good word for Jean Renoir or Marcel Carné they look at you with real pity, as though you've put catchup on your snails.

I met Doris when I spilled my drink on her. "Watch it, Mac," were her first words to me.

You always want to know what women wear, particularly shoes, so (looking at the floor) I see a dark green dress with a collar thing and two (no more) shoes with very high heels, also dark green, and made out of something peculiar—maybe plastic. The panties are regulation and she wore no bra to show that the breasts are better than regulation though somewhat low slung.

"I'm Doris Veering, not Doris Dowling."

I gave her my handkerchief; she mopped her wet sleeve, all the while watching me with enormous dark eyes.

"I didn't think you were Doris Dowling?" You remember Doris Dowling, don't you? She was in *The Lost Weekend* ("thanks but no thanks") and now works in Italian pictures. She has a sister Constance who is also in movies.

NOW

I recall an evening with Doris Dowling in Rome

213

with . . . I can't remember with whom or where yet
I can still see a dark, pleasant, very American girl whose
sister was (or so everyone said) having an affair with
Cesare Pavese.

Last week at lunch with Moravia we talked of those
days. "Pavese was . . . provincial." Moravia shook
his head. To the Italian intellectual the word "provincial" is most complex. As far as I can determine, it
means limited by environment in such a way as to
create all sorts of psychological barriers, not easily
surmounted. The provincial artist (rather like the
American) is forever ill-at-ease with self and work,
unable to reconcile the demands of church, family,
village custom with those of art. In Pavese's case he
finally killed himself and so became a powerful legend
in Italy where the conscience-ridden suicidalist from
the provinces has almost as great an appeal to the public as the mad old exhibitionist who shoots his brains
out has to Americans.

Moravia and I discussed the Dowling sisters. There
were two of them, and one has just died. Pavese's beloved or the other? We try to recall. In the process I
recall that Doris Dowling and I ate goat with a viscous
white sauce in a trattoria. Moravia remarks that Pavese
suffered from premature ejaculation. On my work
table there is a volume of Pavese's letters. I look up
Dowling in the index and find a letter to Doris in
which he tells her that he is at work on a screenplay
which he is calling *The Two Sisters*.

THEN

"They think I look like her in Italy. That's why
I'm here. She's got the business cornered. Though
I tried. God knows I tried. I went to bed with three
directors and a cameraman."

"How were they?"

"The cameraman got me into a Visconti picture but I don't think I'm in the final print which is bad news because I want to be a star, not an actress."

"Sensible." Her nonsequiturs march serenely as to war.

"I believe in telling the truth, don't you?"

I said I had nothing against the truth, as long as it hurt but since she is always so busy telling the truth she missed my nice point. Anyway she ought to be a good person to confide in since she never listens. At least I hope she doesn't, as you'll see.

"I don't suppose you've ever read Marietta Donegal."

I told her that not only had I read her, I was currently being kept by her. This half truth (I've only read part of one of Marietta's sermons about love being *the answer* if only you hold back nothing) made Doris mine.

"You must be a marvelous lover, if *she* is keeping you."

"Yes, I am." What else could I say?

"Unless you're a liar." The dark eyes became narrow; she looked wonderfully stupid, and appealing.

"Come back to the hotel. I'll show you her things. She's away in Turkey. I've even got a carbon copy of her new novel . . ."

"Called?"

"*The Kankered Rose*. It's about man's inability to love."

"Oh, God, she is just great! I read her and read her. She's helped me so much to find myself."

"And me to find you," I said obscurely, but with

215

sufficient catarrh in my voice to make my intention clear.

She has just spoken in her sleep. A loud clear "no." To what, I wonder? I notice one foot which has slipped out from under the sheet. The heel is yellow. You and I are so obscenely rosy that I am drawn to whatever is dark and sallow.

We made love until dawn and I am now feeling pleasantly exhausted, as though never again will I want to make love though I suspect that when she wakes up and has coffee we shall start all over again. I am a great success with her not because of my spirited and crafty performance but because I have been the lover of Marietta Donegal! It's a peculiar situation, to say the least, knowing that the reverent way she holds my prick is not because of me—or it—but because with that fleshly instrument I have probed the high priestess of love.

"Why don't *you* go to bed with Marietta," I finally said when for the dozenth time she allowed that her ecstasy knew no bounds because she was getting what Marietta got.

"I'm not Sapphic!" Doris was quietly proud, and I was delighted, never having heard the word spoken before.

We watched the sun come up together, or rather we saw the sky turn from gray to pale blue just over the Ministry opposite. It was then that we talked seriously. She wanted to know exactly what my relations with Marietta are.

"While she was here, it was fine. Then when she left, it was fine, too."

"You haven't really studied her work, have you?"

"I've studied *her* at close hand." I pulled her onto my stomach. "As close as this." We were lying on

216

the floor looking out the window. Somehow it was a matter of great importance that we help the sun to rise, otherwise eternal night.

"No." She sounded sad but unsurprised. "Men don't get the point to love. Not the way we do."

"It's just the same, I promise." I told her that I had inherited Marietta from V. (she had never heard of him! how furious he would be to know that),

NOW

More furious to find so little mention of me in Eric's notebook. Had I been writing at the same period I would have filled page after page with him.

THEN

and that she went from man to man the same way we go from girl to girl, a regular Donna Joanna she once described herself, though quickly adding, "I'm not interested in conquest for its own sake. I want something much deeper, a sense of breakthrough into another level of being, when the two become one, become whole." Dear God, I can write just like Marietta, and by the yard.

Luckily Doris does not often echo her goddess, but she does hold the same elevated view of sex—are all women this way? are you? I can't think of you as anything but the other half of me and so in all things like. But maybe the sexes *are* different and all those bad—and good—movies which do nothing but notice for a hundred and ten minutes the difference are right.

Strange, come to think of it, how we never discuss our feelings. I always thought the reason for this was our similarity to one another. But now as I write this, listening to the beautiful Doris snore (her "no" was obviously a success in dreamland; she now rests easily), I wonder if we know as little about one another as others know about us.

"It's all the same," I kept telling Doris as we lay together on the floor. Why is it women—maybe most people—hate the idea of not being the only person in the world like themselves? I'm certainly aware that there are others like me—and not just you.

In fact, I have a sense at times of being somebody else. When I was writing about Herostratus I really thought I *was* Herostratus, as if he were telling his story through me. Crazy, I know, and easily explained, psychologically, by the fact that I am an identical twin. Yet Herostratus is so unlike you or me, as far as I know either of us. I shouldn't have thought that I was the sort who would want world fame at any price. Yet I suppose I do want something of me to last. Certainly a thousand years from now someone watching a film of mine will know what it was like to have been with me on a certain day in a certain light . . . the eye dies but what struck the retina remains. I'll settle for that.

NOW

The attraction of old movies is not so much the pleasure one gets in seeing long dead actors come alive as in the glimpses one gets of *real* things: an actual street scene of fifty years ago, with real people hurrying about their business, unaware of the camera, not knowing or caring perhaps that long after they are dead, shadows of themselves at a given time and place can be watched by those who were not even born at that selected moment when Forty-second Street was so urgently crossed at the lunch hour, and preserved on celluloid.

A few years ago I wandered into a Translux newsreel theatre just as an old *March of Time* was being shown. The year was 1935. I watched without much interest until I saw a familiar building: the Department of Commerce in Washington. Then my father appeared on the screen, and I had the sense of sinking without support into the past, nothing to hold onto, like that constant recurring nightmare of being back at school or in the army and no one will believe that one has meanwhile grown up, become a civilian.

I forget the subject of the film. In those days my father was much photographed, usually advancing aviation in Roosevelt's Administration and out. What struck me as he talked to the camera was his youth. The hair which I had known for so many years as white was hardly gray. He was younger than I was watching him. I was both present in the theatre and present in his office (as I looked past him at the room I knew which was the door to the bathroom, and which to the secretary's office, recognized the model planes I used to play with in front of tall windows on whose ledges—out of view—starlings by the thousands lived, etiolating Federal property).

I was both child and man as the film progressed, in two places at once, two continua—and at the end, in a scene showing my father at an airport, I saw with sharp nostalgia that it was high summer in the prewar world, the sort of day on which we would all drive to the Glen Echo amusement park, passing en route a piggery whose smell never failed to horrify and delight me.

THEN

Why is it that whenever women speak of love, I reach not for a gun but my cock? As an offensive weapon, that is, and not as an instrument of fulfillment.

I suppose it is the dislike of being just a thing and despite women's constant talk of their need for a truly meaningful relationship as opposed to the male desire to tear off a quick piece, it is the men who are usually more sentimental or at least more responsive to the whole experience (no matter how brief) than the woman who is thinking not of the man who makes love to her but of the end product of that act, the egg she means to lay. We are at hopeless odds, the two sexes, and ought not to live with one another except for what pleasure can be obtained on those occasions when egg-layer meets cock robin in some neutral nesting place.

Doris believes that there are mysteries to be plumbed in Marietta, too deep for mere man to fathom.

"There is nothing in Marietta but a hair-raising desire to be noticed at any cost. In this very room, in that bed, she told me she wanted nothing less than immortality through her books."

Doris shook dark hair from half-shut eyes; the first pale ray of sunlight struck a pane of glass; together we had made the sun rise. "Marietta Donegal is the feminine principle . . ."

"Like Diana of Ephesus?"

This was ignored, as it ought to have been. What decent American girl has ever heard of the goddess whose temple I burned?

"I think," said Doris drowsily but with some

organization, "that we are all of us reincarnations
—now don't smile like that, I'm serious. You'd believe what I was saying if I talked about hereditary
genes or something repeating from generation to
generation like red hair, well, Marietta is a figure
that continues from generation to generation,
her pattern repeating and repeating down the
ages . . ."

"That's an awful thought. Don't you prefer
the idea of Nirvana? No more personality, no
more . . ."

"What I *prefer* has nothing to do with the way
it *is*." She lay with eyes shut on the floor, speaking
carefully like a priestess translating the words of
deity. "When I first read Marietta I knew that she
was—well, maybe a goddess like your Diana . . ."

She had listened after all; one of those people
who not only talks all the time but tapes mentally
what they can't possibly have heard, in order to
play it back later at some inconvenient moment.

"And I am the same." The priestess crossed her
arms on her chest and looked absurdly attractive.

"The same as Marietta?"

"The same as Marietta. We began with the
human race, and we shall continue to be born
again and again until . . ."

"Until what?"

"Until the end which shall come in fire."

"The monotony doesn't get on your million-
years-old nerves?"

"We breathe thousands of times a day. Does the
monotony of that get on your nerves?"

"On certain days I hold my breath."

"That's why I went to bed with you."

"Because I held my breath?" It is difficult to

know how to deal with a goddess. Marietta preaching her love doctrine was at least standard American: greater effort means greater profits. But Doris is mad as a hatter, and very exciting to me —though not because of that.

"Because Marietta and I are the same, we demand the same sort of lover."

I contemplated this as morning overflowed the windowsill and drowned the room in light.

Doris opened her eyes and looked at me for perhaps the first time. "Someone at the party said you are your twin sister's lover. Is that true?"

"Yes, that is true."

NOW

Curious that incest which was such a major theme in the nineteenth century figures hardly at all in our literature (I have resisted reading Nabokov's recent entertainment on the subject).

Somewhere I once wrote that this might have something to do with housing. In earlier, less crowded times brothers and sisters, parents and children were mysterious and remote to one another. Now, jammed together in small apartments with reverberant walls, they are not only unmysterious to each other but often downright repellent, fellow creators of waste, laundry and irritable scenes.

Significantly, Eric and Erika were, first, twins and, second, brought up in a great house on Long Island where it was possible physically to maintain a distance which, finally, only the act of love could bridge.

I am not surprised.

I find I want to keep writing this phrase over and over again, numbly, for though I am not surprised (the clues have been altogether too obvious in Eric's notebook), at some tribal level I am shocked, responding predictably to ancient tabu. I also find myself wanting to pass judgment, and cannot determine why for I have never had a jealous nature in sexual matters. I have always preferred many partners in various combinations and believed that the world would be considerably happier if others had freed themselves, as I have, of the tribal injunction that it is each man's fate to be paired for life with one woman in order to provide hewers of wood and tillers of soil. But though I do not grudge anyone his appetites, or the variety of his experience, I find myself detesting Eric for revealing what I have from the beginning suspected.

Doris is wrong. Not all truths are liberating. Do I envy Eric for having found the perfect fulfillment of the self-lover, a feminine version of himself? I should like to think not. But twins fascinate me. Can there be loneliness of any kind with a replica of oneself at hand, the mirror's image made flesh? Yet, paradoxically, I have never been attracted to anyone who slightly resembled me. Tabu?

THEN

Doris sat up. The priestess ready to bless a holy alliance, for that is how she regards us. She was overwhelmed. "You've broken through, don't you see? You have made yourself whole!"

"It doesn't seem like that to us." You don't mind my speaking for you—though I know you will mind very much that I have broken our vow never to tell anyone but I couldn't help it or didn't help it and so forgive me. Anyway, Doris is hardly the sort of person people listen to seriously.

I know that doesn't excuse what I have done and frankly I can't think why, lying there on the floor, watching morning come, I told the truth to a crazy girl I've never seen before and may never see again —assuming she ever gets out of my goddamned bed. It is after twelve, and still she snores, dreaming of the feminine principle in which we—I—drown.

"No matter how you rationalize your love for your sister, you have done something marvelous for yourself—for me."

"What's that?"

"I mustn't tell!" The priestess was mischievous. "When did it start?"

"When we were seventeen, at Easthampton, after a party at the Maidstone Club. We got rid of our dates, and walked together in the dunes and then—nothing said—it happened."

"Beautiful!" She was ecstatic (why? I wonder).

"More sandy than beautiful, and painful for her."

"The first time?"

"For both of us. All our lives each had been waiting for the other to make the first move. Finally both moved together—and have moved together ever since. We are one another."

Did I exaggerate? I don't think so—as far as I am concerned. But will you change once you are a wife and mother? Will the egg-laying destroy the idea of us?

I'm suddenly jealous of the child, of Benson. I can't help it. I feel capable of doing something terrible, and perhaps have, telling Doris about us.

NOW

There it is. No, I am not surprised. How could I be? When I have always known the pattern.

I look back over my description of the day at Versailles with Erika and find that my new knowledge of her changes everything. I try to rethink the scene.

Start again.

Skip the description of the garden, tiring to do, and no one will read it. I used to enjoy describing landscapes but nowadays the reader's eye is no longer able to tackle too dense a paragraph, particularly if it is unadorned with proper names or dialogue. "It's my style that's difficult," Mailer said last year, fretting over the relative small sales of his work. I disagreed, partly to tease him for his prose is typically American in the sweaty seriousness with which it is launched at the reader. But he may be right, as if it matters. Simple dialogue in balloons is doubtless the answer.

Erika came toward me. We had not met in fifteen years. Neither smiled. Her face had softened but not aged—well, that's not accurate. The eyes had sunk into the pale face and the mouth turned down at the corners as though she smoked too much which she does not.

"I've become a Roman Catholic." Yes, that was the opening line and my response was "and I was going to say, hello, how are you?" So far so good. She pointed out her French husband. We talked of Benson. The actress who wanted to play Myra came and went. Then Eric.

I send out electrical impulses to the memory bank where all the scenes of a life are kept. Deliberately, I do not look at my first version of the scene.

"How is Eric?"

"I don't see him. I wish he'd marry again."

Something new. I'd not heard the "again" when she first told me, disturbed no doubt by her odd conversational style with its swift declarative sentences and abrupt shifts. So he has been married at least once.

225

I make some joke about Catholicism, not acknowledged.

"Why don't you see Eric?"

"Different worlds." The answer comes much too fast. But I do not follow up, am not suspicious. "He's involved with people who wear beads, you know the kind."

"They must be good subjects to photograph."

"He is interested in spiritualism." All this is suddenly released from the memory bank, like a forgotten deposit showing up on a quarterly statement.

"Marietta's influence?"

"He's gone beyond her. He is inhabited, he thinks, by other people."

"The dead?"

"I don't know. I haven't seen him since I divorced Benson."

"The ghosts drove you away?"

"Yes."

"But he sounds crazy."

"No."

I see a waiter drop a tray on the grass but nothing breaks. I eat half a hard-boiled quail's egg with caviar.

"You had no other children by Benson?" and so on. Nothing new after that. Yet I now know that Eric was married at least once, and that Erika broke with him after her divorce from Benson. "I feel capable of doing something terrible," he wrote twenty years ago. As I recall Erika's stricken face in the green garden light, the glow of the cat's eye rosary in her bag, I know that he finally did it. But what?

THEN

Have not written in the notebook for two days. Much drama, deep depression.

The check from Murray Morris bounced, and so has he—bounced right out of Paris, leaving no forwarding address.

Meanwhile Doris has moved into the hotel and we are playing house. The first thing she did was jimmy open Marietta's two suitcases in order to read all her correspondence (Marietta throws away nothing) and, of course, the typescript of *The Kankered Rose* which Doris thinks a masterpiece, quoting me passages in a thrilling voice, usually having to do with the necessity of unleashing one's feelings, shattering the mind which is the devil that makes us think we're thinking and so on and on and on.

Why am I writing about Marietta and Doris when all I can think of is money and what an idiot I have been?

This afternoon while sitting with Doris at the Flore, counting our traveler's checks (she has two hundred twenty dollars worth, I sixty) and trying to decide where to go and how to live, Clyde R. Bannister Jr and Betty Lou suddenly appeared.

Clyde saw Doris, not me and said, "Hello, there," then saw me and tried to withdraw the greeting but Doris was on her feet kissing him on both cheeks, then she kissed Betty Lou just to be safe, and made them join us. Betty Lou is a fragile blonde who seems to hear an ethereal music we do not.

"Clyde wrote the film I almost did at Warner's last year." Doris looked at Clyde as though she had invented him.

Clyde nodded solemnly. "We wanted you, kid. We were really rooting for you. But the studio wanted a name like Dolores Moran. . . ." There

227

was a moment of silence while we all brooded on the injustice of the studio system. Then just as Betty Lou was about to ask whether or not it was all right to brush your teeth in the tap water, I said, "Clyde, where is Murray?"

"Well, Eric, Murray has this interesting situation going for him in London with Mick Balcon, and he had to leave on short notice."

"Very short, Clyde."

"But our project is still his principal interest, I think I can safely say that."

"Clyde, the check he gave me bounced."

Clyde looked genuinely stricken.

In her little girl voice, it was Betty Lou who spoke for the Bannister family. "I told you not to trust that son of a bitch, Clyde . . ."

"Now, Betty Lou . . ."

"Clyde, he fucked you once before, on the treatment . . ."

"Betty Lou, he paid me . . ."

"A *starvation* wage, he paid you, then he takes the property away and gives it to . . ." She waved a fist full of zircons at me. In a world where everyone is named with each breath, I was nameless. I was hurt.

"I've written my lawyer in New York." I did my best to sound professional, and dangerous. "We're going to sue Murray. He also can't use any of my script until this is straightened out."

That was an error. Clyde made it plain that after giving a lot of thinking to the overall structure his version would not resemble mine at all. "You see, Eric, we've each got our own approach. Also I've been in this racket a long time, and I understand the medium, what you can do and what you can't do. I also understand Murray Morris . . ."

"Shit," said Betty Lou, as though mentioning the name of an old friend of us all.

"Now, Betty Lou . . ."

"What I want to know is how do I get my money?" I asked.

I'm still asking. To make matters worse, Murray actually gave Clyde some money the day he left town—*gave him cash*—and told him to start in. This means that Murray has money and will spend it where he thinks it matters. I don't matter. That's all there is to it. I contemplate murder quite seriously.

On top of all that, Madame Paternault has just brought me a cablegram from Marietta: "Returning tomorrow. Long to see you." Doris is delighted and wants to stay but I know that it's time to go.

"She's very jealous. She would probably try to kill you."

But Doris just looked at me as though I understand nothing about Woman, and maybe I don't. "We have too much in common for that."

"Yes. You have me." I was blunt.

"No. We have ourselves." She reached for the typescript of Marietta's novel but when I threatened to strangle her (notice: three references to murder in as many pages—Murray Morris has shaken me) if she dared read so much as a sentence, she fell with dignity back onto the bed, legs spread wide in order that we might resolve traditionally our very first quarrel.

Now what to do?

I talked to V. this evening; he is on his way to

join Tennessee in London where they are finally putting on *The Glass Menagerie*.

"I could lend you a hundred dollars." He was not very happy at the prospect—and him a best-selling author all summer!

NOW

Even in those days best-selling authors were thought automatically to be millionaires. They were not; or at least I was not. In its first year of publication *The City and the Pillar* earned me some twenty thousand dollars, and—excepting small advances—that was what I had to live on for the next few years.

THEN

I accepted the kind offer, big blue eyes misty with grateful tears (my big blue eyes not his, his are like yellow agates). Then I told him Marietta was coming back. He is about as pleased by this news as I am.

"What're you going to do about that girl in your room—or is it still Marietta's room?"

"Community property, except Marietta pays the rent."

"It's not large enough for three."

"We're going to leave before she comes back. You can take over."

V. made a face. I have never figured out how Marietta got such a hold over him. With everyone, he is as neutral as a cat, with no close connection to anyone except possibly Tennessee and that seems to be just a playful friendship. They improvise funny plays together, and I suppose share certain tastes in common, Marietta not being one.

Tennessee is as mystified as I am by V.'s devotion to her. Mine to her—such as it is—Tennessee could understand because the first time we met he decided that I was a hustler and with a crafty look said, "You should take that old bag for all she's worth."

Is it possible that V. needs someone like Marietta to tell him all about Love and the Mystery of Woman? Attraction of opposites and all that? though I happen to think—and I'm in a minority, I know—that she could learn more from him than he can from her. In his grim way he tries to be honest while she is full of the most horrendous horse shit which Doris has taken up but will soon drop once I get to work on the lovely girl, and she is a wonderful girl even though I don't seem to have captured her for you. But how explain attraction? How record the perfect moment in bed, at lunch, or just coming home at the end of the day to the smell of *pommes frites* mingling with the delicate medicinal odor of opium in the hall?

"How is Erika?" V. always looks uneasy when he mentions you, as well he ought. We've done well in that department.

"The baby will be born in April." I was straightforward. "She's to be married this week."

V. was relieved. "Benson knows?"

"Oh, yes."

"Everything?"

"He knows it's not his."

"I assumed he could count."

I told him a bit about Benson and he grew more cheerful. Somehow the thought of V. married, even to you, or perhaps especially to you, seems all wrong. He is best outside of things. Sometimes I like him, not much but a little.

NOW

Blake's advice "never seek to tell thy love" should not be acted upon. Wanting to be tactful, shrewd—yes, successful—I convinced Eric, early on, that I was indifferent to him and so he responded in kind.

Do I do the same today? Yes. Such patterns are set early and shattered never.

THEN

I told him I was going to just leave, without a word to Marietta.

"That seems the wrong way to go about it."

"Would you enjoy a scene with her at this point, telling her about Doris?"

He twirled the hair over his right ear, making a tight curl, an irritating habit. "No. But you could write a letter. Do something less cold-blooded."

"But we were finished before she went away. Just the way you and she were finished."

"Oh, we're never finished." He didn't sound exactly delighted. "We go on and on no matter what the . . . traffic."

"Well, this roadster is pulling out of the old traffic jam and heading south to Rome. Doris thinks she can get work and I've got a letter to Rossellini."

"She'll be disappointed."

"But not heartbroken . . ."

"No. I don't think you'll figure with the giants . . ."

"She said I was better in bed than D. H. Lawrence."

"She told me the same thing. But then dying men are notoriously bad lays."

We contemplated all the history Marietta had made, not to mention the makers of history. Going to bed with her is like having a part in the chorus of some famous opera, lustily shouting "Alleluia" every time the diva makes her entrance.

After London, V. goes back to the States to see his grandfather. Remember when we went to Washington the first time and were taken to the Capitol where this white-haired old hick was making a speech, and Uncle Reginald said, "That's Senator Gore. He's been blind since he was a child."

NOW

Old hick! It is true my grandfather spoke with a Mississippi accent somewhat modified by the twang of Oklahoma (a state whose first Senator he was, coming to Washington in 1907 at the age of thirty-seven), but he was a superb orator, much in demand on the Chautauqua circuit where he earned his living and at political conventions where he made himself known to the country. His speech seconding the nomination of William Jennings Bryan at Denver in 1908 started what is said to have been the longest demonstration in convention history.

Afterward, as he and the candidate drove off together in a carriage, Bryan said, most solemnly, "You know, Senator, I owe my political success to just three things." "But," and my grandfather would delicately smile at this point, "for the life of me I can't recall what those three things were. I *do* remember wondering what gave him the notion he had been a political success."

In the first year of my life, I arrived at the Senator's house in a basket, and was put to bed in a bureau drawer. Of the various family houses, this is the one I most often dream of, a large gray-stone house set in three acres of wood at the center of Rock Creek Park (it is now the Malaysian Embassy and appropriately altered).

A witty, melancholy man, large-eared, white-haired ("He even *looks* like a Senator," people would whisper when he passed), not fat but with a huge hard stomach. "There must be a watermelon in there," my grandmother would say, not at all displeased by his size for they were Victorians and brought up on eleven-course dinners. "I remember how during the First War, the number of courses at the White House were cut to five." My grandmother was sad, loving food. "What was the nineteenth century like?" I once asked her. "Oh, we ate so well! And there was so much room."

My childhood was spent between the library of the house in Rock Creek Park and the Capitol where I used to roam about in the cellars, committee rooms, even on the floor of the Senate where I sometimes sat in my grandfather's chair while he was in the cloakroom, conspiring against whomever happened to be the President.

"When the Republicans are in, I'm a Democrat. When the Democrats are in, I'm out of step," he used to say, without much satisfaction. He was a Puritan philosopher and found accommodating the "wrong" wicked. He was also a cheerful misogynist: "There is no sound more dreadful than a woman's laugh." He married his wife partly because her speaking voice was bearable. And misanthrope too: "If there was any race other than the human race, I'd go join it."

When I lived in his house I used to join him each

morning in the bathroom while he assembled himself for the day. A complicated ritual because not only did he have to put in upper and lower plates of teeth but one of his eyes was glass and I took exquisite and never-failing pleasure in handing it to him as the high moment of his toilette, the last part of the transformation from frowsy-haired old man who, toothless, spoke, as I once pointed out, "with too much static" to mellifluous statesman and elder of the Republic. Because alone in the family I liked to read, I was his favorite. "Never have children, only grandchildren," he would say, until I almost got married at seventeen, convincing him that his original misanthropy had been justified and the generations of man perfectly irredeemable.

THEN

Just as I was about to go (we were in V.'s room at the back), Hiram Backhouse (pronounced Baykus, who knows why?) sailed in. I don't think you met him, and so are lucky. This summer there have been four attempts on his life. He is what they used to call a remittance man; his family in St. Louis pays him a small amount never to set foot on their side of the Big Mo.

Hiram is about our age with large very green teeth, and a peculiarly loud honking voice. He carries an umbrella rain or shine, cadges drinks at all times of day, usually from strangers who are so fascinated by his sheer awfulness that they gladly give him booze—if they don't, worse luck for them, for his voice raised in denunciation has been known to stop all traffic in St. Germain.

"Your door was open so I came in. I'm not interrupting anything?" He leered at us as he took a bottle of gin from the bureau, and poured himself a shot in a toothbrush glass with the brush still in it. V. turned paler than usual.

"The gin sterilizes the toothbrush." He smacked his lips. "You don't need to worry. I won't catch anything from you, dear."

"Hiram—if you don't mind," V. began but Hiram was ready now for a visit.

"I gather our Southern fried bard has gone to London, forgetting to leave me his half-empty bottles . . . which he promised to do."

"Hiram, we're talking . . ."

But V.'s no match for Hiram who was now happily stirring the gin with the toothbrush. "Putting the make on Eric, dear? Oh, I've seen this developing for some time."

V. was now ready to kill.

I said, "Fuck off, Hiram."

"Always promises, my sweet." Quickly he poured himself more gin; from long experience he knew that his time with us would be short. "You do make a pretty couple, no doubt of that, like two boys in the sort of vulgar fiction you-know-who writes."

"Get your ass out of here." Any attack on *The City and the Pillar* always sends V.'s blood pressure up. I suppose because he knows it isn't very good.

"Temper, temper!" Hiram's green teeth flashed. "You really should work harder, and read more. I'll lend you my Ph.D. thesis if you like. It was much admired at Northwestern—so was I until I was rusticated or urbinated, as it turned out. The subject was 'How the Spaniel Figures in the Novels of George Eliot.' Of course, you've never read her —too busy writing when you should've been reading—but it was I who made the discovery that in each book not only is there a spaniel but the angel

dog—they are all glorified such was her vision—
invariably turns the plot at a crucial moment, as in
Silas Marner when the dog is *not* petted by the
young squire at the start of the novel, demonstrating to both dog and us that the young man's nature
is unloving. In *Felix Holt the Radical*, however, it
is a different story . . . oh, dear, I'm boring you.
I can tell. You don't like dogs, do you? or literature.
I should've known . . ."

V. looked at me and I looked at him. Then with
a concerted movement, each took one of Hiram's
arms, lifted him off the floor, threw him out the
door onto the landing where he settled with a
crash, still holding the glass of gin unspilled. V.
slammed and bolted the door.

"You know," he said grimly, "that in Turkey
Hiram was thrown in jail and that after two weeks
they released him, unable to bear him. A Turkish
jail!"

There was a rap at the door. "My dears, I left
my umbrella." V. opened the door and threw the
umbrella at Hiram who ducked with long practice.
"You don't have any more gin, do you?" he asked
as the door again slammed in his face.

NOW

That is the end of the red notebook. I put it down on
the coffee table and try to recall what happened next.

Eric left Paris without a word to me or anyone else.
According to Madame Paternault he and Doris had
vanished a few days after the Hiram Backhouse inci-
dent. "They leave as though they had not paid the
bill," said Madame somewhat mystified, "but the room
was being paid for by Madame Donegal so . . ." She
could not understand Eric's stealth but I did. He had

received a second wire from Marietta, to say that she would be returning sooner than expected, and so he fled, leaving the red notebook, and Marietta.

I have a memory of Marietta at about that time. We were sitting on metal chairs in the Tuileries gardens, watching children sail toy boats in the round pond at the center. She was in mauve, with a scarlet belt—she is drawn to exotic colors the same way that in her prose she prefers the unusual word to the merely familiar, relying, I fear, more on her sensory memory of the word than on its actual dull, dictionary meaning. Like Nabokov, she sometimes has a wanton way with our difficult language, and like him often booby-traps her own meaning with the carefully selected wrong word.

At Marietta's request, I told her everything I could about Doris Veering. She smoked a hashish cigarette as I talked, eyes turned without love upon the playing children.

"Of course," she said when I had run out of details, "I'm glad for him."

"Are you really?"

The talent for self-deception was as superb then as now. "He must find himself. I did what I could. I always do. I think you know that."

I let this slip by, another flower petal in the swift bright river of her life. "She's pleasant enough, and marvelous-looking." This was the sort of detail that invariably causes Marietta's broad forehead to fill with fine horizontal lines. "But she seems a bit of a nut: the wisdom of the east, that sort of thing."

"But I like that. After all, Eric has a psychic side to him. Now don't laugh. Simply because you repress that side of yourself doesn't mean it's not there."

"*What's* not there?" This is the sort of statement

which makes *my* forehead wrinkle with irritation and bewilderment.

"The magic dimension. The true core . . ."

"Please. Don't . . ."

"But it is there."

"Even though *it* cannot be put into words?"

"Not easily. Why do you think I write so many books?"

I accepted the question as rhetorical and did not answer.

"Because I must give to others that sense of the numinous I have. And with each book I think—now at last it's clear but of course it never is, there is always so much more to say, to feel, to discover. The mysteries within mysteries."

I stopped listening, made designs with the pebbles at my feet, thought of Egypt's Valley of the Kings which I had seen for the first time that spring, and had there been overwhelmed by a sense of the past, and the knowledge that there is no mystery at all about our estate despite the beautiful progression of the Book of the Dead, despite Marietta and her talk of *it*. We come and we go and the time between is all that we have. I am stoic, and can be nothing else.

At times I envy the conceit of Marietta—of Eric, too, perhaps—that they matter hugely in eternity as well as time and that there are marvels yet to be revealed involving, oh, crucially! continuation of personality after death. And I feel a villain whenever I say that there are plenty more where we came from (even Eric suspected as much), while the end of the whole race is now not only possible, but probably at hand. Yet to say such things is to be thought cruel, and certain to evoke the response of the wife in Gide's *Immoralist* when, at her urging, the husband describes his pederastic life, and she cries, "How dare you tell me the truth!"

"I had thought *you* would get Eric when I left." She paid me back for my praise of Doris's beauty.

"No. Erika was my consolation prize."

"By the way, he left a notebook in the room, with a note to Madame Paternault, asking her to mail it to his sister."

"Have you read what he wrote?"

"No." I suspect this was true. "It's a sort of journal." Then she acknowledged my indiscretion. "You and Erika?"

"Yes. She's being married—or is just married—to a man called Benson."

"Robert L., a businessman, interested in books?"

"Yes. Did you know him?"

Marietta nodded, the love goddess smile hovering archaically upon her lips.

"Erika is pregnant."

Marietta looked at me sharply. "By you?"

"Yes." I could not resist the . . . what? Boast, I suppose.

Marietta seemed not at all sure what her reaction ought to be. Needless to say, when it came, it was in perfect character. "*I* could never have a child," she began solemnly one of her most elaborate speeches which, on at least one occasion, lasted an hour as she examined with total fascination the extraordinary fact of her physical barrenness which had, luckily, been compensated for not only by a fecund literary genius but by an ability to love *totally* and (though she would never admit to anything so practical) without fear of conception—particularly in the pre-Pill era when she was first born of the sea at San Diego, and invented love.

I recall nothing else of that day, or time. The pebbles at my feet which I had formed into a cairn. The mauve and scarlet of her clothes. The smell of hashish burning. The children at the round pond sailing paper ships. The pleasing thought that I would be father to a child come April, and the puzzled second thought: why should I care? The world was over-crowded even then. Famine spreads; wars begin; we may yet see the end of us for nothing wise will now be done ("Oh, yes, Malthus," smiles the intelligent father of four, as though the name Malthus, so long discredited, somehow reveals the problem as a slight one, easily solved by sea farming or the turning of petroleum into food).

Nevertheless, in adding to the population one Eric Benson, I am atavistically pleased with myself for have I not continued in him—and unknown to him—not only that long line of Alpine warriors and priests (all right, most were apothecaries) but that splendid ferocious line of Anglo-Irish preachers and politicians (a Mississippi saying: "The Gores are brilliant folk, but they got no sense") who together created me as I have created him, crossing my bloodline with Erika's? and though I have helped to crowd this dying world, I find myself stupidly pleased at the thought and follow his career as best I can, wondering what sort of person he is—and would we get on? I think so. After all, my father was the only man I ever entirely liked so perhaps Eric and I could have relived a similar relationship (forty-three years without a quarrel, though without much agreement: my father voted for Goldwater, to my despair).

So ends that summer of twenty-one years ago. Eric vanished, with Doris. Marietta about to take up with Derek or Guido or Benjamin. I to return to the States, life devoted to achieving some balance between furious vision and a talent still unformed. Erika to give birth the first week in April at Southampton to my son.

Just as the cannon on the Gianiculo went off to celebrate the fact of noon, Marietta arrived wearing a vast Chinese coolie hat. At the door she said, significantly, "Well!"

Then, arranged in a chair with a full light upon her face and a glimpse of the dome of Sant' Andrea della Valle through vines, she again said, "Well."

"I've read it all."

"The screenplay?"

"Yes. Not possible."

"But you are doing *Julian* and Fellini has done the *Satyricon* and . . ."

"Forget about it."

"You're not exactly helpful." She looked at me with the hurt expression of a member of the Trinity confronting a nonbeliever.

"I'm sorry. Not that it isn't interesting. I think I understand Eric for the first time."

"Oh, that." For a moment she had quite lost interest in her old love, her mind on the screenplay and its possible sale. Then she recalled herself. "Yes, one does know him better now." Marietta was again love goddess, compassionate, forgiving, all-encompassing—nothing masculine alien to her.

"Did he marry Doris?"

"That actress? No. Did you know that she stole the manuscript of *The Kankered Rose*—just a carbon but even so—and years later had the nerve to ask me to autograph it?"

"Which you did."

"What else could I do? She is still devoted to my

work and lives in Santa Monica, doing little theatre work. She is quite ugly now." Marietta smiled reflexively. I recall my grandmother's maid who, catching her looking bleakly into a hand mirror, said, "Time do blast us all." Except Marietta who has blasted time.

"But did he marry?"

Marietta nodded. "Twice. I met the second wife. She was just like his sister."

"We don't need to examine that."

"I saw her only once. Saw him only once after Paris. It was when I was speaking at a university near Monterrey, in northern California. When I finished—a wonderful audience, by the way, you should get out and meet the young more, they are *the* audience—"

"Except they can't read."

"You perhaps, but they love my work, at least the interesting ones do."

"I'm glad."

"Anyway there was Eric at the back of the room with, I thought at first, Erika. But it turned out to be the wife; a quiet girl, perfectly pleasant. Anyway, I went to their place for a drink and he told me that they were involved in all sorts of psychic research and that he planned to make a movie based on the idea of possession . . ."

"I think he really thought he was Herostratus."

"Yes, he did. And I think he was. For a time. Oh, I know how skeptical you are, how much you hate the idea of such things but there are strange forces in the world that cannot be explained. I have always had a sense of having lived before, of things repeating . . ."

I stopped myself from saying that at her age everything was repetition. Instead: "If it gives people pleasure to believe they are inhabited by ghosts, I see no harm in it."

243

"Oh, but you do! You've always been so . . . censorious. Everything must be examined in the most unflattering light." She put up one long hand to shield her face from a sudden ray of sunlight. I closed the shutter. "You refuse to acknowledge any magic in life, anything miraculous like love . . ."

"I wish I was like you." The irony was not total.

"You would be happier."

"I'm sure of that. What ghost inhabits you at the present?"

"You see? There you go, reducing the marvelous to a joke."

"I'm sorry. I didn't mean to make it sound as if you were some sort of hotel with ghosts checking in and out but . . ."

"It's not like that." She was growing irritated but I could not stop.

"I'm sure it's not. So tell me what it *is* like."

She looked at me suspiciously. I made my face a blank the way one does just before the television camera's light goes on.

"There is a sense of not being alone. Of holding within one's mind another personality. After all, what is art? What is invention but a release of ghosts upon the page? Our reflection of one another . . ."

" 'Each man bears the entire form of man's estate.' " I quoted Montaigne more accurately than usual, though I cannot think why since old books are no longer relevant in these swinging times. Before yesterday nothing.

"I believe, as Eric believed, that the vibrations set off by a life never stop, that the spirit of someone long dead can still inhabit a sympathetic mind . . ."

"Well."

"I know what you think. Even so, I've always felt that you were really a sensitive like me. But with your passion for what you call the rational you've never opened up, never allowed another mind the opportunity of communicating."

"I shouldn't mind Voltaire paying me a visit but with my luck I would probably get your friend D. H. Lawrence and he would stay on forever, nagging."

"You could do worse. But have you really *never* felt the presence of someone else in your mind?"

"Never. In fact I am not always certain that my own mind is at home."

"Don't joke. I'm serious, even if you're not."

"I do dream of dead friends."

"What do they say?"

"Nothing memorable. But it is curious that the one thing they have in common is *not* knowing they're dead. I always have to remind them . . ."

"Naturally." She was sharp.

"Well, it gives us something to talk about. Usually they ignore it . . ."

"Because they know they're eternal, even if you don't."

"Possibly. John Latouche was particularly angry when I asked him what he was doing up and around since he'd been buried a dozen years ago. He tried to explain but then the sound went off. It was like a silent movie. He shook a fist at me, very odd. Oh, then," I was now in the spirit of the thing, "last summer I saw Lord Byron at Pisa. I was looking for the palazzo where he lived and as I walked down a narrow street, parallel to the Lungarno, Byron and a friend came out of an alleyway. Byron was fat, and wore a tight brown jacket, and rather unusual flapping slippers, perhaps Turkish.

He was talking intently to a thin sallow man, smaller than he. As I approached, they vanished. Then I stepped into the alleyway from which they'd come and found myself—naturally—at the palazzo where he'd lived."

Not certain whether or not I was making fun of her, Marietta returned to the subject of Eric. "We got on very well that evening. He was more relaxed than in the old days . . ."

"Did either of you mention the notebook?"

"No. I suspect he'd forgotten it and I'd not read it then . . ."

"Really?"

"Well, I'd *looked* at it when I found it in the room but I never actually read it straight through until this spring when I was selling all my papers to the University of Texas, including your letters, by the way . . ."

"I've *given* yours to the University of Wisconsin."

Marietta took this in usual stride. "And found the notebook in an old suitcase that I'd forgotten about. Then when I heard he was dead, I decided to try to sell the screenplay. He did owe me quite a lot of money."

"I wish I could help you." We looked at one another.

Then I made my last and fatal move. "Now you know all about Erika and me."

She smiled, looked young; she can still suggest a girl when delighted; she was delighted now. "You know why Eric fell out with his sister?"

"Did he?"

"Oh, yes. He was responsible for Benson divorcing her. I saw Benson not long ago—we were friends, you know, years ago, before the war—and he told me everything. Apparently Eric was jealous of Benson, felt that he had lost Erika. Anyway he came to spend a weekend with them at Water Mill, such a pretty house —for sale now but I can't afford it—and the subject of the child came up . . ."

"My contribution to the population explosion."

"Yes. Only the child isn't yours. It was Eric's. I suppose he was drunk. Or on some drug. Whatever, he told Benson everything. How he and Erika had been lovers for years, how the child was his—apparently she wore a diaphragm that night with you. Anyway by the time he'd finished, the marriage was over. Benson was horrified, and Erika tried to kill herself. Or so I've been told."

Marrietta looked at me, like fate. "Imagine waiting all those years and then, suddenly, destroying a marriage, and two . . . three? lives."

Marietta's work was now complete. Whatever demon inhabits her presently (is it Eric himself?) can be regarded as a total success. I have now no son, and the line stops here.

Marietta was not quite finished. "I thought it very wicked of the two of them, making you believe you were the father all these years. But then, poor children, they were desperate. I mean they had to pick *someone*. I think Eric suffered for what he did."

"In what way?"

"There is a certain mystery about the way he died."

"He fell from a building, you said."

"He was photographing a riot, yes. And he fell . . . but it is also possible that he jumped."

"What makes you think so?"

"There was no film in the camera." Marietta got to her feet. She put the red notebook into her embroidered handbag. "I must go."

At the door we kissed chastely like old lovers.

"Was there any autopsy? He might have been on drugs."

"Autopsy? Didn't I tell you? He fell into a *burning* house. There was no body, only some melted dental work. The widow promptly remarried, someone rich from Pasadena. Good-by."

So at the end, fire. What else? For the three of us and all the others, too, when time stops and the fiery beast falls upon itself to begin again as dust-filled wind, without memory or you, Herostratus.